Financial Management
Information Systems
and Open Budget Data

A WORLD BANK STUDY

Financial Management Information Systems and Open Budget Data

Do Governments Report on Where the Money Goes?

THE WORLD BANK
Washington, D.C.

Contents

Box

Figures

Financial Management Information Systems and Open Budget Data
http://dx.doi.org/10.1596/978-1-4648-0083-2

Maps

Tables

Preface

Financial Management Information Systems and Open Budget Data: Do Governments Report on Where the Money Goes? is a World Bank Study, initiated in 2012 after an extended stocktaking exercise, to explore the effects of financial management information systems (FMIS) on publishing reliable open budget data, and to identify potential improvements in budget transparency. A rich data set was created by visiting the government public finance (PF) websites in 198 economies, and collecting evidence on the use of 176 FMIS platforms in publishing open budget data.

This study is not intended to develop another index or ranking on budget transparency. The scope is limited to the budget data disclosed by the governments on the web for the details of budget revenues and expenditures, as well as the results achieved. Other important aspects of fiscal discipline and transparency, related to a wide range of extrabudgetary funds, assets, contingent liabilities, and quasi-fiscal operations were not possible to detect through such an external review. A number of key indicators linked with disclosing budget data were defined and measured using a simple scoring scheme.

The main findings are explained in several categories to highlight the important aspects of publishing reliable and meaningful open budget data, and present some of the good practices. Guidelines for publishing reliable open data from FMIS solutions are presented to share options for improving budget transparency. Finally, web links to relevant PF sites and FMIS platforms are presented through the FMIS World Map.

Target Audience

World Bank teams, government officials, and other specialists involved in FMIS and Open Budget Data projects.

Objective

Governments' disclosure of PF information from reliable FMIS databases can improve transparency and accountability, if the data posted on their websites are accurate, easily accessible, and meaningful to citizens. This study reports on the availability, source, reliability, and integrity of the budget data published from FMIS, identifies good practices, and provides guidelines on publishing reliable open budget data to assist in exploring the effects of FMIS on budget transparency.

Activities

Oct 2012	Initiation of activity (P143587—Effects of FMIS on Budget Transparency).
Nov 2012	Concept review (approved on November 28, 2012).
Jan 2013	Data collection for a new data set on FMIS and Open Budget Data (scanning the PF-related websites in 198 economies) was completed (as an extended stocktaking exercise, building on an earlier database developed in mid-2012).
Jan 2013	FMIS World Map beta version was updated (the first release posted in June 2010) to present the web links to 176 FMIS platforms from 198 economies on Google Maps.
Apr 2013	Initial findings and data set were shared with government officials and task teams/managers for possible improvements in the data set and results.
Jun 2013	Decision meeting (June 19, 2013).
Jul 2013	Final report was delivered as a World Bank Study.

Key Resources

Hyperlinks (Uniform Resource Locators—URLs) to related web sources are shown as underlined text.

- The FMIS and Open Budget Data—data set (July 2013 version). Available from the FMIS Community of Practice website (https://eteam.worldbank.org/FMIS).
- Cem Dener, Joanna A. Watkins, and William L. Dorotinsky, *Financial Management Information Systems: 25 Years of World Bank Experience on What Works and What Doesn't*, World Bank Study, April 2011.

Acknowledgments

This paper was prepared by the Governance and Public Sector Management Practice (PRMPS) of the World Bank's Poverty Reduction and Economic Management (PREM) Network.

The principal authors of this study, Cem Dener and Saw Young (Sandy) Min (PRMPS), would like to acknowledge the World Bank staff involved in the preparation of this document: Birgül Meta for her valuable contributions during the preparation of the new data set for assessing the impact of FMIS on budget transparency; Angela Lisulo for her support during the early stages of data collection; and Jeffrey N. Lecksell, Cartographer, the World Bank Map Design Unit, for reproducing the map on the cover page.

Special thanks to the PEFA Secretariat for their valuable support with the comparative analysis of our findings with the complete set of PEFA indicators, and to Joanna A. Watkins for her useful comments on the definitions and key findings. We also benefited from the practical suggestions and guidance of Jim Brumby, Young Kyu Kang, Adrian Fozzard, and Nick Manning in developing this study, as well as the comments of Vivek Srivastava, Verena Maria Fritz, Anupama Dokeniya, Maritza A. Rodriguez, Gert Van Der Linde, Leif Jensen, Paolo de Renzio, and Amparo Ballivian on the final report. Finally, we would like to thank Stephen Knack and Ivor Beazley (concept note stage), as well as Nicola J. Smithers, Vivek Ramkumar (OBI/IBP), Xavier Rame (IMF), and Marijn Verhoeven, for their invaluable peer review comments.

The short-term consultancy services related to this study were funded from the Korean Trust Fund.

About the Authors

Cem Dener is a senior public sector specialist within the Governance and Public Sector Management practice of the Poverty Reduction and Economic Management network. Since 2004, he has been working on the improvement of public financial management practices, and the development of Financial Management Information System (FMIS) solutions in all regions. He is one of the authors of the World Bank's FMIS Study (April 2011). He is also involved in the organization of regional knowledge sharing and learning events and the formation of communities of practice. He received BSME from METU, Ankara, Turkey (1982), MSc from Cranfield Institute of Technology, Bedford, United Kingdom (1985), and PhD from Vrije Universiteit Brussel, Belgium (1992), working on modeling complex systems.

Saw Young (Sandy) Min is a Junior Professional Officer with the Governance and Public Sector Management practice of the Poverty Reduction and Economic Management network. She is focusing on fiscal/budget transparency and public financial management and is a core member of the Global Initiative for Fiscal Transparency. She co-authored a case study on the public participation in the budget process in the Republic of Korea and contributed to the publication, *Beyond the Annual Budget: Global Experience with Medium Term Expenditure Frameworks.* She holds an MPA from Cornell University and is currently pursuing a PhD in Public Finance at George Mason University.

Abbreviations

AFR	Africa Region
APEC	Asia-Pacific Economic Co-operation
BC	Budget classification
CoA	Chart of accounts
COFOG	Classification of the Functions of Government (UN)
COTS	Commercial off-the-shelf software
CSV	Comma-Separated Values (file storing tabular data in plain-text form)
DOC	Microsoft Word document format
EAP	East Asia and Pacific Region
ECA	Europe and Central Asia Region
EGDI	e-Government Development Index
e-Gov	Electronic Government (e-Government)
FMIS	Financial management information system(s)
FT	Fiscal transparency
GFSM	Government Finance Statistics Manual 2001 (IMF)
GIFT	Global Initiative for Fiscal Transparency
HIC	High-income country
IBP	International Budget Partnership
ICT	Information and communication technology
IFMIS	Integrated financial management information system
KML	Keyhole Markup Language
LCR	Latin America and Caribbean Region
LDSW	Locally developed software
LIC	Low-income country
LMIC	Lower-middle-income country
MNA	Middle East and North Africa Region
MoF	Ministry of Finance
MTBF	Medium-term budgeting framework

MTEF	Medium-term expenditure framework
MTFF	Medium-term fiscal framework
MTPF	Medium-term performance framework
OBD	Open budget data
OBI	Open Budget Index
OBS	Open Budget Survey
ODF	Open Document Format (an open standard since 2006)
OECD	Organisation for Economic Co-operation and Development
OGP	Open Government Partnership
OLAP	Online analytical processing
OLTP	Online transaction processing
OSS	Open source software
PDF	Portable Document Format (an open standard since 2008)
PEFA	Public Expenditure and Financial Accountability
PF	Public finance
PFM	Public financial management
PPT	Microsoft PowerPoint presentation file
PREM	Poverty Reduction and Economic Management Network
PRMPS	PREM Governance and Public Sector Management Practice
RDF	Resource Description Framework
SAR	South Asia Region
TS	Treasury system
UMIC	Upper-middle-income country
WWW	World Wide Web
XLS	Microsoft Excel file format for storing tabular data
XML	Extensible Markup Language (an open standard since 1998)

Executive Summary

Financial Management Information Systems and Open Budget Data

Do Governments Report on Where the Money Goes?

In recent years, the topics of budget transparency and open data have been increasingly discussed. Most discussants agree that for true transparency, it is important not only that governments publish budget data on websites, but that the data they disclose are meaningful and provide a full picture of their financial activities to the public. Most governments have made substantial investments in capacity building and technology for the development of financial management information systems (FMIS). The question is, how much of the disclosed information and documents are reliable? What is the scope of disclosed information? Is there any reliable information about important aspects of fiscal discipline and transparency?

Civil society groups and international organizations have developed a number of fiscal transparency instruments and guidelines to evaluate the existence, regularity, and contents of certain key budget documents published in the public domain and assess whether the information complies with international standards. However, these instruments do not concentrate on the source and reliability of published information, or on the integrity of underlying systems and databases from which governments extract data.

Guidance on publishing reliable open budget data from underlying FMIS solutions is scarce. This study is the first attempt to explore the effects of FMIS on publishing open budget data, identify potential improvements in budget transparency, and provide some guidance on the effective use of FMIS platforms to publish open budget data.

> If the public finance information published on government websites is to be reliable, relevant budget data should ideally be obtained from dependable FMIS platforms and should comply with open data standards.[1]

Five key research questions guided this study:

1. What are the important characteristics of current government web publishing platforms designed for the disclosure of budget data?
2. Is there any evidence on the reliability of open budget data published from FMIS?
3. Are there good practices demonstrating the effects of open budget data from FMIS in improving budget transparency?
4. Why is a "single version of the truth" difficult to achieve in the budget domain?
5. Can there be some guidelines to improve practices in publishing reliable open budget data from FMIS?

The conceptual framework used in this study has several important bases:

▸ Several decades of experience in the development of FMIS solutions in all regions.
▸ Evidence that the reliability and accuracy of government budget data depends on the capabilities and integrity of underlying FMIS platforms.
▸ Existence of proven industry standards for publishing open government data.
▸ Growing demand from citizens for improved budget transparency, accountability, and participation.
▸ Widespread use of the Internet and web technologies for transforming the public sector management.

> The study is designed to draw the attention of governments to possible improvements in the accuracy, timeliness, and reliability of budget reporting, simply by publishing on public finance websites open budget data that are drawn from underlying FMIS platforms.

Methodology

In line with the research questions of this study, 20 key and 20 informative indicators were identified to assess the status of government websites for publishing open budget data from FMIS. A rich data set was created by visiting the public finance (PF) websites (mainly those of Finance Ministries or Departments) in 198 economies, and using these indicators to collect evidence on the use of 176 FMIS solutions in publishing open budget data. For the purposes of this study, the team focused only on websites that present information on the governments' budget operations. A score was assigned for each of the key indicators.

Using the total scores from the 20 key indicators, the researchers categorized the websites in four groups according to the good practices observed: A=Highly visible; B=Visible; C=Limited visibility; D=Minimal visibility. A survey form was used to share the initial findings with relevant government officials for their validation and feedback on possible improvements (through e-mail exchanges). The results were presented through a comparative analysis of regional and income-level patterns, and through correlation with relevant budget transparency indices.

The team identified the government PF websites that displayed good practices and innovative solutions, and created an interactive geospatial map to share important results broadly in a user-friendly format. Guidelines for publishing open budget data from FMIS were also developed to help governments and practitioners improve their websites and open data practices.

Main Findings

Despite the widespread availability of 176 FMIS platforms used by 198 governments around the world, good practices in presenting open budget data from reliable FMIS solutions are highly visible in only 24 countries (12 %).

The average score for the performance of 198 governments in publishing open budget data from FMIS is 45.1 out of 100, based on the 20 key indicators. About 93 websites (presenting extensive or significant information) appear to be benefiting from underlying information systems while publishing PF data, but most of these do not yet provide open data.

Overall, there are only 48 countries (24 %) where civil society and citizens have the opportunity to benefit from PF information published on the web (Citizens Budget and transparency portals) to monitor the budget and hold their governments accountable. In many countries, external audit organizations do not appear to be using the FMIS platforms effectively for monitoring the government's financial activities or auditing the budget results.

Governments in high- and middle-income economies publish budget data dynamically in various formats, mainly from centralized systems, while many lower-income economies tend to publish static budget data, mostly through documents posted on PF websites. By Region, ECA, LCR, SAR, and EAP appear to perform better in terms of posting budget reports from databases, while MNA and AFR tend to publish static budget reports through PDF files. A large number of governments in AFR do not have PF publication websites.

To verify whether the findings of the study are consistent with key observations from other fiscal transparency indices, the distribution of FMIS & OBD scores was compared with such fiscal transparency instruments as Public Expenditure and Financial Accountability (PEFA), Open Budget Index (OBI), and UN e-Government Development Rankings. It was found that the patterns are largely similar, and the FMIS & OBD scores correlate positively with the PEFA indicators and OBI scores.

The researchers identified 100 cases from various government websites in 53 countries (from all Regions and income levels) to highlight some of the good practices in different areas of publishing open budget data from FMIS.

Guidelines

Drawing on the observations of this study, the lessons learned from good practice cases, and experience in the development of FMIS solutions and open budget data portals, the team developed a set of guiding principles for government officials, citizens and civil society groups, and oversight agencies to use in improving government practices for publishing open budget data through FMIS platforms.

▶ Availability of timely and comprehensive budget information

There should be dedicated government PF websites that provide timely and regular information on budget plans and execution results. The completeness of published PF information (including off-budget fiscal and quasi-fiscal operations, as well as assets and contingent liabilities), and the presentation of budget execution performance through time-series data, are very important.

▶ Disclosure of details about underlying information systems

Government PF websites should present the key features of underlying information systems, promoting the use of interoperability standards and digital signature, and disclosing data protection and information security policies to build confidence in underlying information systems and relevant ICT practices.

▶ Availability of user-defined (dynamic) query and reporting capabilities

Government PF websites should have capabilities for interactive multidimensional data analysis with flexible and user-friendly dynamic query and reporting options, and the consistency of historical data should be ensured.

▶ Publishing reliable and interlinked open budget data

Publishing open budget data (free, online, editable) from FMIS or data warehouse solutions often requires a change in the culture of organizations. Governments can benefit from the various guidelines on publishing "linked open data" to maximize the benefits. The use of open budget data also creates opportunities to add value to public information.

▶ Authentication of the sources of public finance data

Inclusion of the system name and a date/time stamp on published reports is one of the key indicators for the reliability and integrity of underlying information systems. Appropriate safeguards should be implemented to protect data from unauthorized modification and access, and oversight mechanisms should be in place to ensure the reliability and integrity of systems, the security of operations, and the effectiveness of IT governance and oversight functions.

▶ Improving the quality of presentation

Interactive data visualization options, graphical user interfaces, feedback mechanisms, advanced search/reporting options, innovative tools (searchable interactive maps of PF information), broadened access to PF data through mobile applications, and the provision of daily updates on key performance indicators all substantially improve the quality of presentation in PF websites.

▶ Promoting the effective use of open budget data

Publishing meaningful open data on budget revenues, spending, and other financial activities is crucial for any government to explain how the public money has been spent. The Citizens Budget is an important instrument to achieve this. Open budget data portals can also be used to support the participatory budgeting process, in which people in a locality or community can jointly decide on priorities in the government's budget and monitor implementation. The results of participatory budgeting, gender focus, or citizen-led expenditure monitoring should be visible in PF websites. Finally, the oversight agencies should benefit from PF web platforms and underlying systems as much as possible, for effective monitoring and assessment of the government's financial activities.

Conclusions

So, can we see where the money goes? The study shows that only a small group of countries provide good access to reliable open budget data from underlying FMIS solutions. Many governments publish substantial information on their PF websites, but the contents are (not always) meaningful to provide adequate answers to the question, "Where does the money go?" Therefore, the main conclusion of this study is that when it comes to government PF websites, **what you see**

> Selected cases demonstrate that even in difficult settings, innovative solutions to publish open budget data and improve budget transparency can be developed rapidly, with a modest investment, if there is commitment from the government and strong interest from the public.

is (not always) what you get. Many governments need to make additional efforts that will build confidence in the budget data they disclose. As citizens and civil society increasingly demand access to open data about all financial activities, governments around the world are trying to respond to this democratic pressure.

The outputs of this study are expected to provide a comprehensive view of the status of government practices for publishing budget data around the world, and to promote debates around the improvement of PF web publishing platforms to support transparency, accountability, and participation by disclosing reliable information about all financial activities. Future research could explore such important aspects as capturing and posting additional data on other financial activities, and learning more about user perceptions.

Note

1. *Public finance* information covers all *public sector* revenues, expenditures, assets and liabilities. *Budget data* includes mainly *general government* revenues and expenditures. *Dependable FMIS platforms* are subject to regular IT audits to ensure the reliability and integrity of systems, the security of operations, and the effectiveness of IT governance and oversight functions. *Open data* are accessible to the public (online) in editable (machine-readable) and reusable format, without any restriction (free/legally open).

CHAPTER 1

Introduction

Governments around the world are at various stages of implementing public financial management (PFM) reforms, designed to improve the strategic allocation of resources (to promote growth and reduce poverty), operational efficiency (to minimize waste and align spending with revenues), and fiscal discipline (to improve the credibility of the budget). As part of this effort, most have made substantial investments in capacity building and technology for the development of financial management information systems (FMIS).

Within the last decade, the use of FMIS has become a critical part of improving budget transparency. Disclosure of public finance (PF) information to citizens through FMIS platforms can improve transparency, if the published budget data are accurate, easily accessible, and meaningful. Fiscal transparency in turn can improve trust in government, if the public interprets the motives for publishing the open budget data positively and the transparency is maintained for long periods. However, designing robust FMIS solutions to capture all financial activities and publish open budget data, and measuring the effects of FMIS on budget transparency, continue to be major challenges.

There is no widely accepted framework for assessing the quality of web publishing or the performance of the information systems that are used as a basis for recording and reporting open budget data. Core PFM diagnostic studies[1] typically analyze government resource allocations within and among sectors, and assess the equity, efficiency, and effectiveness of those allocations in the context of the country's macroeconomic framework and sector priorities. However, the indicators defined for these assessments are inadequate to check such aspects as the source and reliability of information.

> If the PF information published on government websites is to be reliable, relevant budget data should ideally be obtained from dependable FMIS platforms and should comply with open data standards.

While most governments have FMIS that are capable of providing useful budget data, it is not clear to what extent the budget data are published on dedicated websites, with dynamic links to reliable systems for consistent and timely disclosure of information in easy-to-understand and machine-readable formats. Also, the scope, completeness, and quality of the PF information vary considerably, and there seems to be no widely used guidance on improving the reliability and reusability of budget data. This study is designed to shed light on these less known areas, and to report the findings, together with a geospatial mapping of the results, to explore the effects of FMIS on publishing open data. Although it is well known that the use of open budget data can contribute to improving accountability and transparency, reducing corruption, and enhancing citizens' trust in government (see Figure 1.1), it is beyond the scope of this study to look at these aspects.

This exercise addresses several key questions:

1. What are the important characteristics of current government web publishing platforms designed for the disclosure of budget data?
2. Is there any evidence on the reliability of open budget data published from FMIS?
3. Are there good practices demonstrating the effects of open budget data from FMIS in improving budget transparency?
4. Why is a "single version of the truth" difficult to achieve in the budget domain?
5. Can there be some guidelines to improve practices in publishing reliable open budget data from FMIS?

This study is divided into six chapters. Chapter 1 covers the rationale and aims of the study, and definitions used, along with a summary of relevant budget transparency indices and standards. Chapter 2 explains the methodology used to identify the important aspects of disclosing open budget data, as well as the simple

Figure 1.1 Potential effects of publishing reliable open budget data from FMIS

FMIS:
• Record all revenue and expenditure transactions daily

▶ Publish open budget data through FMIS:
• online
• editable/reusable
• searchable
• free/legally open

▶ Potential improvements in budget transparency by posting:
• reliable
• timely
• accurate
• meaningful public finance information

▶ Building trust in government's financial activities by:
• sustaining transparency
• demonstrating meaningful results
• publishing open budget data from dependable FMIS

Source: World Bank data.
Note: FMIS = financial management information system.

scoring scheme used to categorize current government practices in publishing open budget data from FMIS. Chapter 3 presents the data collected from 198 economies and describes general patterns observed in publishing budget data. Chapter 4 highlights some of the good practices in publishing reliable and meaningful budget data through FMIS, and provides a geospatial mapping of the results. Chapter 5 presents the guidelines suggested for possible improvements in government practices to publish open budget data through FMIS platforms. Chapter 6 summarizes the key findings and presents the conclusions of this study. Appendixes A–C amplify the information in the study, and Appendix D lists the feedback providers for the study. Bibliography and open data references are presented at the end of the study.

Definitions

Broadly speaking, *financial management information systems* are the automation solutions that enable governments to plan, execute, and monitor the budget. Modern FMIS platforms help governments comply with financial regulations and reporting standards, and support decentralized budget operations through centralized web-based information and communication technology (ICT) solutions. FMIS platforms also facilitate the disclosure of PF information to citizens to improve budget transparency, government accountability, and participation. Figure 1.2 illustrates the core FMIS functions and their interrelationships.

Whenever FMIS and other PFM information systems (for example, e-Procurement, payroll, debt management) are linked with a central data warehouse (DW) to record and report all daily financial transactions, offering reliable consolidated results for budget analysis, decision support, performance monitoring, and web publishing, these platforms can be referred to as *integrated FMIS* (or IFMIS). IFMIS solutions are rare in practice, and to avoid unrealistic expectations, the term should not be used as a synonym for core FMIS functionality.

Next-generation IFMIS solutions combine PFM operational systems for *online transaction processing* (OLTP) with powerful DW capabilities for multidimensional *online analytical processing* (OLAP) to assist in effective forecasting, planning, performance monitoring, and decision support (see Figure 1.3). Innovative IFMIS solutions also allow more detailed analysis by providing dynamic query options to a large number of users, both internal (public organizations) and external (citizens, nongovernmental organizations, businesses), and they support the publication of *open budget data*.

For the purposes of this study, *open budget data* (OBD) is defined as the government budget data that are made accessible to the public (online) in editable (machine-readable) and reusable format, without any restriction (free/legally open). Requirements to protect the confidentiality of personal or classified information should be considered while posting open budget data.

Public finance (PF) *information* includes the budget data plus other components of the government's financial activities (for example, extrabudgetary funds, tax expenditures, quasi-fiscal activities, fixed assets, contingent liabilities). This study is designed to capture evidence on the disclosure of *budget data* only.

Figure 1.2 Core FMIS functions and interfaces with other PFM systems

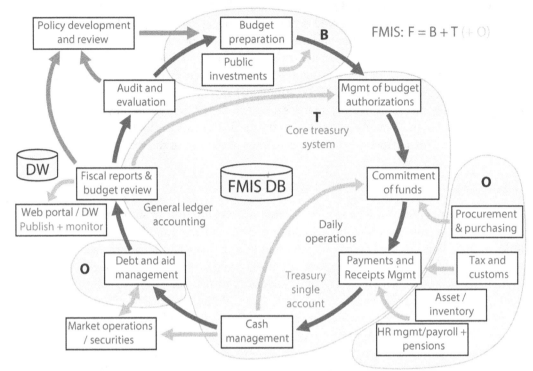

Source: World Bank data.

Note: For the purposes of this report, FMIS (**F**) is defined narrowly to include mainly core budget preparation (**B**) and treasury/budget execution (**T**) systems, complemented by other (**O**) modules in some cases. Arrows are used to indicate the linkages between core modules (blue), the interfaces with other systems (gray), as well as the links with policy development and review processes (red). The core FMIS functions and their contributions to PFM practices are more fully explained in Dener, Watkins, and Dorotinsky, 2011. FMIS DB = financial management information system database; DW = data warehouse; HR = human resources.

Fiscal transparency (FT) is defined as the ready availability of meaningful information on fiscal policy and achievements to the public. Budget transparency refers to the full disclosure of budget data on government revenues, allocations, and expenditures (ideally for the whole public sector).

Trust in government is defined as the public's overall assessment of the government's current entitlement to enforce its policy decisions, laws, and regulations based on past performance and the view of how the government and its institutions are likely to act in the future (Box 1.1).

An IFMIS can be considered as a complex system—that is, a network of heterogeneous components that interact nonlinearly, to give rise to emergent behavior; emergence is the way complex systems and patterns arise out of a multiplicity of relatively simple interactions. Such information systems exhibit "organized complexity," and the main challenge is to integrate a limited number of interlinked PFM functions through a centralized web-based platform that supports countrywide decentralized operations, and provides innovative tools for decision support, performance monitoring, and web publishing.

Figure 1.3 Key components of integrated FMIS solutions combining OLTP and OLAP

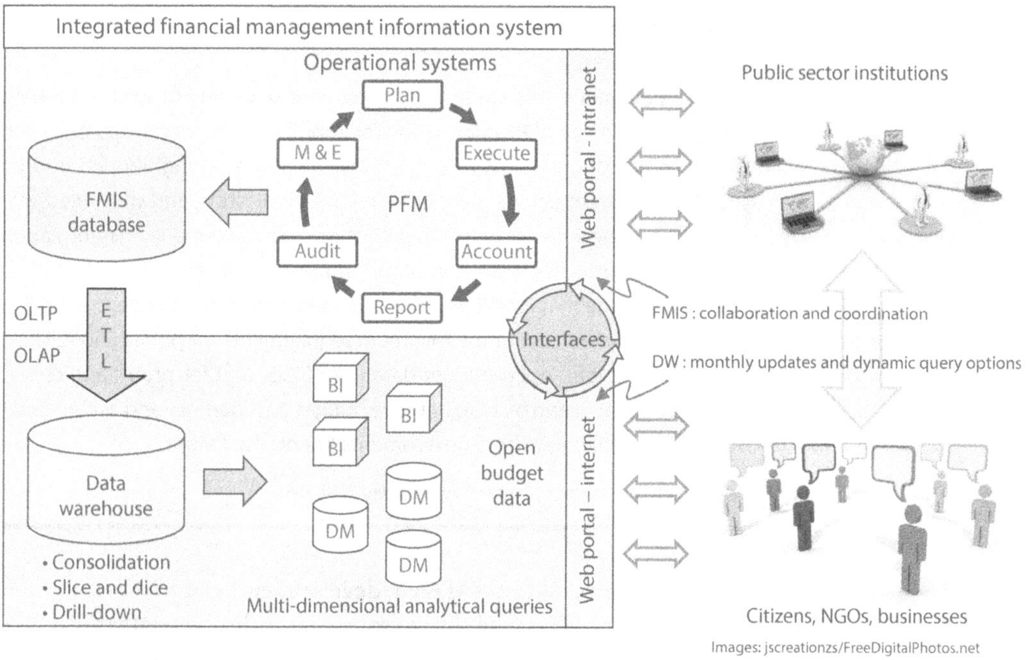

Source: World Bank data.
Note: OLTP = online transaction processing; OLAP = online analytical processing; FMIS = Financial Management Information System; PFM = Public Financial Management; DW = Data Warehouse; NGO = Nongovernmental organization; ETL = extract, transform, load; BI = business intelligence; and DM = data mining.

Box 1.1 Trust in Government

Trust in government is a multidimensional concept in which citizens expect the government and public officials to be responsive, honest, and competent, "even in the absence of constant scrutiny."[a] Trends in trust have been closely examined by recent studies, often with a sense of alarm regarding a potential long-term decline of confidence in governments. However, little work has been done to understand and empirically measure the drivers of trust in public institutions.

As Manning, Shepherd, and Guerrero (2010) highlighted in a working paper, while the concept of trust in government is clearly important, there are some major definitional problems and associated questions about the strength of any metrics that can be used to capture it. Terms such as *performance, trust, legitimacy,* and *trustworthiness* are often used interchangeably, or at least with meanings that are very specific to the particular situation. Various measures of trust in government that result from surveys are often unclear about the unit of analysis (what is being trusted?) and whether respondents understood trust or confidence in the same way as the interviewers. The assumption made in the working paper is that views of government performance draw on assessments of the past; views of the trustworthiness of public institutions require an estimate about the future; and views on trust and legitimacy

box continues next page

---

draw on both of these and are about a current assessment of government—against general and specific criteria respectively.

Considering these definitions, this study assesses current government web publishing practices related to the disclosure of PF information for improving budget transparency and accountability. The use of FMIS solutions to publish reliable and meaningful open budget data was analyzed from different perspectives using relevant indicators, and substantial evidence was collected about the linkages between published data and underlying information systems, as well as the platforms designed to improve budget transparency.

The study does not assume that FMIS has a direct influence on trust in government. The assumption is that if governments meet the minimum requirements for publishing reliable, timely, accurate, and meaningful open budget data from FMIS, and for promoting citizen participation, these good practices may help improve budget transparency and accountability, and thus contribute to building trust in governments' financial activities.

a. Miller and Listhaug 1990, cited in Manning, Shepherd, and Guerrero 2010, 358.

Open source is an approach to the design, development, and free distribution of software, offering practical accessibility to source code. In the context of FMIS modernization/development and open source solutions, *innovations* refer to improvements on existing ways of doing things, whereas *inventions* change the way things are done. *Open data/content licensing* schemes and *open data catalogues*, which can be used for publishing open data and knowledge, are visible in many government websites.[2]

Budget Transparency Instruments: Overview

In recent years, the discussion of data openness has been gaining momentum on the global stage. For example, a number of countries and organizations are engaged in discussions of the challenge of collecting and disclosing timely and reliable information about budget operations, extrabudgetary funds, and quasi-fiscal activities.[3] The International Budget Partnership (IBP) is one of the largest forums for these discussions.

The World Bank has adopted a proactive and committed stance in the discussion of data openness by participating in the process, as well as advocating for it in collaboration with other development partners. In April 2010, the Bank made its development data available for download free of charge.[4] The Open Development Technology Alliance[5] (also known as the ICT Knowledge Platform) was created to enhance accountability and improve the delivery and quality of public services through technology-enabled citizen engagement (for example, using mobile phones, interactive mapping, and social media).

The discussions on open government data, and more specifically on budget transparency, are of particular interest to the Governance and Public Sector Management Practice (PRMPS) of the World Bank's Poverty Reduction and

Economic Management (PREM) Network. The World Bank is one of the international financial institutions taking the lead in the Global Initiative for Fiscal Transparency (GIFT), an initiative that promotes budget transparency, public participation, and accountability globally.[6]

BOOST is another useful tool developed by the World Bank for transforming detailed government expenditure data from FMIS databases into an easy-to-understand data set (XLS) for detailed analysis through pivot tables and geomapping tools. Expenditure data can be combined with information on public institutions, service delivery, and households to facilitate rigorous expenditure analysis.

A number of fiscal transparency instruments have been developed within the last decade (Appendix C provides an overview). These instruments can be grouped in three categories according to their functions (Table 1.1).

Most of these instruments are designed to evaluate the existence, regularity, and contents of certain key budget documents published in the public domain, as well as the mechanisms for public access. However, they do not examine the source, reliability, quality, and readability of the PF information that governments publish governments on the web—a major gap.

Another important challenge is the difficulty in comparing open budget data published by governments in different formats. In February 2012, the IBP published the Open Budget Survey 2012,[7] which revealed that most governments do not meet basic standards of transparency and accountability with their national budgets.

The signing of an Open Data Charter by G-8 leaders on June 18, 2013, is an important development to promote transparency, innovation, and accountability. The charter sets out five strategic principles that all G8 members have endorsed: an expectation that governments will publish data openly by default, along with

Table 1.1 A summary of fiscal transparency instruments

#	Fiscal Transparency Instruments	# of countries	Since	Last update
	A. Surveys and indices			
1	Open Budget Index (OBI)	100	2006	2012
2	PEFA PFM Assessment	121 (public: 65)	2005	—
3	IMF Fiscal Transparency ROSC	93	1999	—
4	Global Integrity Index	119	2004	—
5	Right to Information Index	93	2011	2011
6	UN e-Government Survey and Rankings	193	2003	2012
	B. Standards and norms			
7	IMF Code of Good Practices on FT	n.a.	1998	2007
8	OECD Best Practices for Budget Transparency	n.a.	2002	—
	C. Fiscal transparency initiatives			
9	Global Initiative for Fiscal Transparency (GIFT)	n.a.	2011	—
10	Open Government Partnership (OGP)	55 (+5)	2011	—

Source: World Bank data.
Note: Data retrieved in June 2013. PEFA = Public Expenditure and Financial Accountability; PFM = Public Financial Management; IMF = International Monetary Fund; FT = Fiscal Transparency; OECD = Organisation for Economic Co-operation and Development; — = not available; n.a. = not applicable.

principles to increase the quality, quantity, and reuse of the data that are released. G8 members also identified 14 high-value areas (including "Finance and Contracts") in which they will release data. Each member of the G8 is expected to publish an open data action plan by October 2013, showing how it will make more data available, in line with the charter and its principles. Additionally, the Lough Erne Declaration from the G8 Summit sets out agreed principles for the future, of which one is related to the open data: "Governments should publish information on laws, budgets, spending, national statistics, elections and government contracts in a way that is easy to read and reuse, so that citizens can hold them to account." These developments in the area of open data highlight the importance of ensuring the reliability of published data and the integrity of the underlying systems.

Good practice cases have shown that the success of open government data projects relies heavily on strong political commitment, skills development, technology platforms, and resources, as well as on demand from citizens and civil society. Although there have been encouraging developments and some successes in this area, there are still challenges that need to be overcome if the public is to reap the full benefits of open data.

Notes

1. Public Expenditure Reviews; Public Expenditure and Financial Accountability (PEFA) Assessments.
2. The Open Definition sets out principles to define "openness" in relation to data and content. Creative Commons licenses enable the sharing and use of creativity and knowledge through free legal tools. Data Catalogs website presents a comprehensive list of open data catalogs in the world.
3. http://www.data.gov/opendatasites.
4. The World Bank Open Data portal: http://data.worldbank.org
5. Open Development Technology Alliance is a joint initiative anchored by the World Bank Institute and the ICT Sector Unit and supported by other Bank Networks/Regions.
6. IMF's Fiscal Transparency website includes relevant links: http://www.imf.org/external/np/fad/trans.
7. Open Budget Survey 2012, www.openbudgetindex.org.

CHAPTER 2

Methodology

 I
Definition of indicators

 II
Data collection

 III
Data analysis

 IV
Validation of observations

 V
Results reporting

 VI
Preparation of guidelines

To measure and analyze the effects of financial management information systems (FMIS) on publishing reliable open budget data, the team used a six-part approach:

Definition of Indicators

The first step was to identify the key indicators (*questions*) for collecting data about the characteristics of current web publishing platforms, and the metrics (*points*) for measuring government practices for publishing open budget data from FMIS. The *indicators* were defined in two categories for assessing the effects of FMIS on publishing open budget data:

- Key indicators: 20 indicators were derived from 10 factual questions about the source, scope, and reliability of open budget data.
- Informative indicators: 20 indicators were derived from 10 questions providing useful information about other important features.

Each indicator is linked with one of the subcomponents of the questions listed below. The details of all questions, subcomponents, and indicators are provided in Appendix A. The questions corresponding to each indicator are also shown in Table 2.1 (for Example, I-1 is linked with question Q1.3).

Table 2.1 Key and informative indicators and points assigned

Ind	Q	Key indicators	Points
		Existence of dedicated website for publishing PF data	
I-1	Q1.3	Is there a dedicated website for publishing PF information?	0/2
I-2	Q2.1	Is there a website/document about the FMIS platform?	0/2
		Source and reliability of open budget data	
I-3	Q3.1	What is the source of PF data?	0/3
I-4	Q3.3	Presence of open budget data (online, editable/reusable, free)	0/1
I-5	Q3.5	Is system name visible in dynamic/static reports?	0/1
I-6	Q3.6	Is system time stamp visible in dynamic/static reports?	0/1
		Scope and presentation of PF information	
I-7	Q4.1	Quality: What is the quality of PF data presentation?	0/2
I-8	Q4.2	Content: Is there a sufficient level of detail?	0/1
I-9	Q4.3	Are the budget results presented easy to understand (Citizens Budget)?	0/2
I-10	Q5.1	Are the BC/CoA details published?	0/1
		Contents and regularity of PF information	
I-11	Q6.1	Is the approved annual budget published?	0/1
I-12	Q6.2	If yes: Regularity of publishing annual budget plans	0/1
I-13	Q7.1	Are MTEF documents published?	0/1
I-14	Q7.2	If yes: Regularity of publishing MTEF plans	0/1
I-15	Q8.1	Are public investment plans published?	0/1
I-16	Q8.2	If yes: Regularity of publishing investment plans	0/1
I-17	Q9.1	Are budget execution reports published?	0/1
I-18	Q9.3	If yes: Regularity of publishing budget execution reports	0/1
I-19	Q10.1	Is the external audit of central government budget operations published?	0/1
I-20	Q10.2	If yes: Regularity of publishing external audit reports	0/1

Inf	Q	Informative indicators	Points
I-21	Q11.1	Public expenditures > Consolidated budget reports published?	0/1
I-22	Q11.2	Public expenditures > Sector analysis published?	0/1
I-23	Q11.3	Public expenditures > Regional analysis published?	0/1
I-24	Q11.4	Public expenditures > Gender analysis published?	0/1
I-25	Q11.5	Public expenditures > Analysis of spending for children & youth published?	0/1
I-26	Q11.6	Public expenditures > Debt data published?	0/1
I-27	Q11.7	Public expenditures > Foreign aid/grants published?	0/1
I-28	Q11.8	Public expenditures > Fiscal data on state/local governments published?	0/1
I-29	Q11.9	Public expenditures > Financial statements published?	0/1
I-30	Q11.10	Public expenditures > Public procurement and contracts published?	0/1
I-31	Q12.1	Is there an open government/open budget website?	0/1
I-32	Q13.1	Does FMIS support the PFM needs of state/local governments?	0/2
I-33	Q14.1	Is there a harmonized public accounting system for all budget levels?	0/1
I-34	Q15.1	Are PF data published on the Statistics website? Or another website?	0/3
I-35	Q16.1	Is access to information explained?	0/1
I-36	Q17.1	Are PFM roles and responsibilities clearly explained?	0/1
I-37	Q18.1	Compliance with specific international reporting standards?	0/1

table continues next page

Table 2.1 Key and informative indicators and points assigned (continued)

Ind	Q	Key indicators	Points
I-38	Q19.1	Web statistics (reports on website traffic)?	0/1
I-39	Q19.2	Which platforms are available for providing feedback?	0/3
I-40	Q20.1	What languages are used to publish PF information?	—

Source: World Bank data.
Note: FMIS = Financial Management Information System; PF = Public Finance; BC = Budget Classification; CoA= Chart of Accounts; MTEF = Medium-Term Expenditure Framework; PFM = Public Finance Management; — = not available.

Questions for Key Indicators

Q1. Does the Finance Ministry/Department have a website or portal that is dedicated to publishing public finance (PF) information?

Q2. Is there a website or document describing the web-based FMIS platform?

Q3. What is the source of the PF information that is published on the web?

Q4. Is the PF information meaningful to citizens or budget entities?

Q5. Is the data structure or full listing of budget classification (BC)/chart of accounts (CoA) published?

Q6. Are documents associated with annual budget plans published?

Q7. Are documents associated with medium-term expenditure framework (MTEF)[1] published?

Q8. Are documents associated with public investment/capital budget plans[2] published?

Q9. Are documents associated with budget execution published?

Q10. Are documents associated with the external audit of central government budget operations published?

Questions for Informative Indicators

Q11. What is the level of detail of the public expenditure/revenue information published online (plans versus actuals, sectoral or regional details, and so on)?

Q12. Is there a dedicated website for open government/open budget initiatives?

Q13. Is there a web-based application supporting the Public Finance Management (PFM) needs of state/provincial governments or municipalities as a part of the FMIS?

Q14. Is there a harmonized public accounting system supporting all budget levels (unified budget classification and/or chart of accounts)?

Q15. Are there duplicate government budget reporting websites other than that of the Finance Ministry/Department (for example, Office of Statistics)?

Q16. Is there a web page explaining the policy/regulations for access to PF information, web publishing standards, or frequency of PF reporting?

Q17. Is there a web page with links to regulations[3] for clarifying the PFM roles and responsibilities?

Q18. Are published PF data compliant with the IMF Government Finance Statistics (GFS)and/or UN Classification of the Functions of Government (COFOG) standards?[4]

Q19. Is there a web page for receiving feedback on PF information/user satisfaction, or for presenting web statistics?

Q20. What languages are used to publish the PF information online for external viewers?

The metrics (*points*) linked with the *20 key indicators* were used to measure the current status of government practices for publishing PF data (Table 2.1). Points were linked with the response options (ranging from 0 to 3) for each indicator. The sum of all points (Σ Point) was normalized to obtain a total *score* (from 0 to 100), reflecting the strength of each country's platforms for publishing open budget data from FMIS or other sources:

$$\frac{\Sigma_{20}^{1} \; Point}{\Sigma_{20}^{1} \; Max \; Point} \times 100 = Score$$

Most of the key indicators (31 of 40) were measured using a simple point scheme (0 or 1) to ensure the collection of consistent responses by all reviewers and avoid ambiguities in interpreting related evidence. Informative indicators were included to complement the data set by providing additional feedback on ease of access to information, compliance with some of the widely used PF reporting standards, and presentation options.

The total score was used to identify the *group* of each country, for a comparative analysis of current government practices and the clarification of regional and income level patterns, as explained under the "data analysis" section.

Data Collection

To explore the effects of FMIS on budget transparency, the team[5] created a comprehensive *data set* (worksheet with linked data) by reviewing government PF websites (usually maintained by the Ministry of Finance or other relevant public entities) and collecting *evidence* (web links/URLs and relevant documents/reposts) about the source and reliability of PF information published through FMIS or other platforms.

Responses to all questions were obtained directly from the websites by three reviewers. Almost all indicators/questions are designed to measure important characteristics of web publishing platforms (source, reliability, dynamic query options, and so on), and the patterns for publishing PF data (scope, frequency, regularity, and so on), using evidence visible on the websites.

The *FMIS and Open Budget Data (FMIS & OBD) data set* contains five components for capturing a number of additional fields related to basic data, FMIS solutions, and other relevant indicators, in addition to the key and informative indicators (scores and evidence). Additional information collected about the FMIS solutions (scope, years in operation, type of application software, technology architecture, and so on) and relevant web links are included to provide more comprehensive feedback on existing systems.

The composition of the data set is summarized in Figure 2.1.

Financial Management Information Systems and Open Budget Data
http://dx.doi.org/10.1596/978-1-4648-0083-2

Figure 2.1 Composition of the FMIS & OBD data set

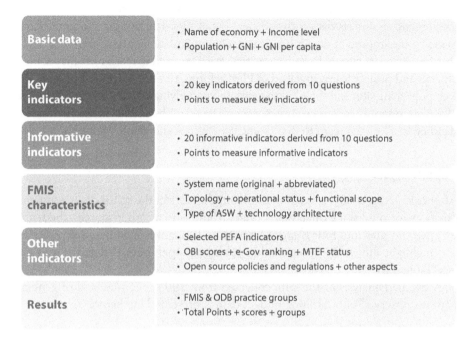

Basic data	• Name of economy + income level • Population + GNI + GNI per capita
Key indicators	• 20 key indicators derived from 10 questions • Points to measure key indicators
Informative indicators	• 20 informative indicators derived from 10 questions • Points to measure informative indicators
FMIS characteristics	• System name (original + abbreviated) • Topology + operational status + functional scope • Type of ASW + technology architecture
Other indicators	• Selected PEFA indicators • OBI scores + e-Gov ranking + MTEF status • Open source policies and regulations + other aspects
Results	• FMIS & ODB practice groups • Total Points + scores + groups

Source: World Bank data.
Note: PEFA = Public Expenditure and Financial Accountability; MTEF = Medium-term expenditure framework; OBI = Open budget Index; FMIS = Financial management information system.

All key and informative indicators are explained in Appendix A, and all other data set components are described in Appendix B.

Most of the questions are designed to measure observable facts about the contents of relevant PF publication websites, and the reviewers used a well-coordinated approach to check the existence of various features consistently. Only Q4 partially reflects the opinions of the reviewers, based on specific criteria for "quality" and "content." These questions were included as a measure of the initial perception of first-time visitors to the PF websites about the presentation of budget data and the level of detail visible at first sight. Thus, questions Q4.1 (Quality) and Q4.2 (Content) reflect the assessments of external reviewers of whatever is visible on the home page of the main PF publication sites, and Q4.3 highlights the scope of publications related with the Citizens Budget.

Obviously, because these responses are based on the initial perceptions of three reviewers, there is a risk of missing website features that may not be so obvious at first glance. However, since the reviewers visited all PF-related websites from the 198 economies at least twice, they believe that the collected evidence and scores will provide useful feedback on the status of relevant government practices.

To overcome the difficulties of screening a large number of web pages prepared in national languages, the reviewers used the Google Chrome web browser and available machine translation options while visiting government PF websites. In most cases the quality of translation was good enough to understand the contents of the website, check the source and reliability of published PF information, and view the contents of reports/data with sufficient detail. Nevertheless, the team may have missed some important details because machine translation options were not available for several languages. In such cases, the reviewers tried to reach relevant country officials and project teams involved in PFM reforms, to clarify various aspects of PF web publishing sites and their linkage with the underlying systems. Eventually, most of the important PF related websites were screened with a sufficient level of understanding to allow the team to draw some conclusions and identify patterns.

Data Analysis

After calculating total *scores* (from 0 to 100) that reflect the status of government practices for publishing open budget data from FMIS or other sources, the team mapped the sites into four *groups* (A to D) to distinguish good country practices and highlight innovative solutions for publishing open budget data from FMIS (see Table 2.2).

A detailed analysis of the data collected from 198 economies, and of general patterns observed in publishing budget data is presented in chapter 3.

Validation of Observations

The findings of this stocktaking exercise were shared with relevant government officials to check the evidence collected, reflect other perspectives, and improve the accuracy of observations. Country-specific survey forms were automatically created from the data set to share the initial findings, and relevant government officials were invited to provide feedback. Responses received from 43 governments were used to improve the data set and collected evidence.

To identify and promote exemplary country systems and good practices supporting budget transparency, the team also selectively contacted particular countries to learn more about government practices with regard to publishing budget data on PF websites, and to clarify the reliability and integrity of underlying FMIS databases.

Table 2.2 Definition of FMIS & OBD groups to map the status of government practices

Group	Score	Current status	Description of relevant government practices
A	75–100	Highly visible	Extensive information; FMIS is used to publish timely open data; easy to navigate; dynamic query options.
B	50–74	Visible	Significant information; FMIS rarely used to publish open data; static web pages updated regularly.
C	25–49	Limited visibility	Some information; ongoing activities to improve the web content or publish open budget data on the web.
D	0–24	Minimal visibility	Minimum or no information; no Finance Ministry/Department website or budget data.

Source: World Bank data.
Note: *FMIS = Financial Management Information System.*

Results Reporting

The team then recorded their observations and findings about each key indicator (see chapter 3). To verify whether the findings of the study are consistent with key observations from other fiscal transparency indices, the distribution of FMIS & OBD scores was compared with such fiscal transparency instruments as Public Expenditure and Financial Accountability (PEFA), Open Budget Index (OBI), and UN e-Government Development Rankings. Finally, the team developed an overview of some of the good practices in publishing reliable and meaningful budget data, and a geospatial mapping of the results (FMIS World Map) on Google Maps (see chapter 4). The FMIS World Map will be updated annually to ensure the visibility of the findings and provide easy and open public access to good practices.

Preparation of Guidelines

As the last step in this study, the team prepared some guidelines to highlight the important aspects for improving the reliability and integrity of PF information sources and the presentation and quality of budget data published. These guidelines are intended to help governments improve how they publish PF information, and to encourage those that show little or no visibility of PF information on the web by laying out some of the achievable good practices. Chapter 5 presents these guidelines.

Notes

1. The MTEF consists of three stages: (1) medium-term fiscal framework (MTFF); (2) medium-term budget framework (MTBF); and (3) medium-term performance framework (MTPF).
2. This indicator is used to highlight the publication of investment plans published separately (not embedded in the annual budget or the national development plan/strategy).
3. Online availability of regulations, organic budget law, procurement law,and so on.
4. IMF GFS: International Monetary Fund Government Finance Statistics. UN COFOG: United Nations Classification of the Functions of Government.
5. The three website reviewers were Ms. Saw Young (Sandy) Min, Ms. Birgül Meta, and Mr. Cem Dener.

Financial Management Information Systems and Open Budget Data
http://dx.doi.org/10.1596/978-1-4648-0083-2

CHAPTER 3

Data

This chapter presents the descriptive data analysis based on a rich data set created by visiting the government websites in 198 economies, and collecting evidence on the use of 176 financial management information system (FMIS) platforms in publishing budget data.

Status of Government Practices in Publishing Open Budget Data

The current status of government practices in publishing open budget data is presented in four *groups*, derived from the *scores* calculated through 20 key indicators (Table 3.1).

> Open budget data from reliable FMIS solutions are highly visible in only about 24 economies out of 198 reviewed (12 %).

In most cases, the lack of timely and meaningful budget data may be an indication of ineffective budget monitoring or greater opportunities for the misuse of funds. Substantial improvements in budget transparency could be achieved simply by publishing reliable open budget data from FMIS or other databases on existing government websites, if there is political will and commitment.

Web publishing practices vary significantly among the different Regions of the World Bank and among countries of different income levels (see Figure 3.1). Among the 198 public finance (PF) websites assessed, the average score assigned by the team was 45.1 out of 100. About 69 PF websites (35 %) provide significant budget information, but only a small portion of this information qualifies as open budget data from FMIS. Forty-five governments (23 %) provide minimal or no budget information on the web; and 60 governments (30 %) provide some information, mostly from archived documents without enough evidence on the use of FMIS databases as the source of the PF data.

Table 3.1 A summary of current government practices in publishing open budget data

Group ▶	Good practices in disclosing OBD from FMIS	Economies	% E	Regions	%R
A	Highly visible (extensive information)	**24**	12 %	**16**	10 %
	Argentina; Australia; Brazil; Colombia; Ecuador; El Salvador; Germany; Guatemala; India; Ireland; Rep. of Korea; Mexico; The Netherlands; New Zealand; Nicaragua; Paraguay; Peru; Russian Federation; Singapore; Slovenia; Spain; Turkey; United Kingdom; United States				
B	Visible (significant information)	**69**	35 %	**57**	34 %
	Afghanistan; Albania; Armenia; Austria; Bahrain; Bangladesh; Belgium; Bhutan; Bolivia; Bosnia and Herzegovina; Bulgaria; Canada; Cape Verde; Chile; China; Croatia; Czech Republic; Denmark; Dominican Republic; Estonia; Finland; France; Gabon; Georgia; Ghana; Honduras; Hong Kong SAR; Iceland; Indonesia; Italy; Japan; Jordan; Kenya; Kyrgyz Republic; Latvia; Lebanon; Lithuania; Macedonia, FYR; Madagascar; Malaysia; Malta; Mauritius; Moldova; Morocco; Namibia; Nepal; Norway; Pakistan; Philippines; Poland; Portugal; Romania; Serbia; Slovak Republic; Solomon Islands; South Africa; Sri Lanka; Sweden; Switzerland; Tanzania; Thailand; Timor-Leste; Tonga; Uganda; Ukraine; Uruguay; Venezuela; RB; Vietnam; Zambia				
C	Limited visibility (some information)	**60**	30 %	**56**	33 %
	Algeria; Andorra; Angola; Antigua and Barbuda; Azerbaijan; Bahamas; The; Belarus; Botswana; Burkina Faso; Cambodia; Taiwan, China; Costa Rica; Côte d'Ivoire; Cyprus; Djibouti; Dominica; Egypt; Ethiopia; Fiji; Gambia; Greece; Grenada; Guinea-Bissau; Guyana; Haiti; Hungary; Iraq; Israel; Jamaica; Kazakhstan; Kosovo; Lao PDR; Lesotho; Liberia; Luxembourg; Macao SAR; Malawi; Maldives; Mauritania; Micronesia; Mongolia; Mozambique; Nigeria; Oman; Panama; Papua New Guinea; Rwanda; Samoa; Saudi Arabia; Senegal; Sierra Leone; St. Lucia; Swaziland; Tajikistan; Trinidad and Tobago; Tunisia; United Arab Emirates; West Bank and Gaza; Yemen; Zimbabwe				
D	Minimal visibility (minimal or no information)	**45**	23 %	**39**	23 %
	Barbados; Belize; Benin; Brunei Darussalam; Burundi; Cameroon; Central African Republic; Chad; Comoros; Congo; Congo, Dem. Rep.; Cuba; Equatorial Guinea; Eritrea; Guinea; Iran, Islamic Rep.,; Kiribati; Korea Dem. Rep.; Kuwait; Libya; Liechtenstein; Mali; Marshall Islands; Monaco; Yugoslavia; former; Myanmar; Nauru; Niger; Palau; Qatar; San Marino; São Tomé and Principe; Seychelles; Somalia; South Sudan; St. Kitts and Nevis; St. Vincent and the Grenadines; Sudan; Suriname; Syrian Arab Republic; Togo; Turkmenistan; Tuvalu; Uzbekistan; Vanuatu				
	Totals >	**198**		**168**	

Source: World Bank data.
Note: The 198 *"economies"* include all 188 of the World Bank member countries, plus some of the large economies (from European Union [EU], Organisation for Economic Co-operation and Development [OECD], and Asia-Pacific Economic Co-operation [APEC] members). The *"Regions"* include 168 World Bank member *countries* that are currently receiving advisory and financial support to implement public sector management reforms.

Income level. Although high-income countries (HICs) tend to publish budget data regularly (32 out of 54, or 59 %, are in group A or B), most of these economies do not present evidence about the source of open budget data on their websites. Most upper-middle-income (UMICs) and lower-middle-income countries (LMICs) follow similar patterns. Most of the low-income countries (LICs) have limited or no visibility in terms of publishing budget data (29 out of 38, or 76 %, are in group C or D). Of the 35 fragile states, 29 (83 %) are in group C or D, with little or no visibility on the web in terms of publishing PF information.

Regional distribution. Among the Regions, the Europe and Central Asia (ECA), Latin America and the Caribbean (LCR), East Asia and the Pacific (EAP), and South Asia (SAR) countries show a large number of good practices in publishing extensive/substantial information (45–50 % of countries in these

Figure 3.1 Current status of government practices in publishing OBD from FMIS

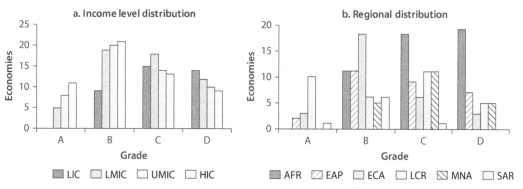

Source: World Bank data.
Note: LIC = Low-Income Country; LMIC = Lower-Middle-Income Country; UMIC = Upper-Middle-Income Country; HIC = High-Income Country. AFR = Africa Region, EAP = East Asia and Pacific Region; ECA = Europe and Central Asia Region; LCR = Latin America and Caribbean Region; MNA = Middle East and North Africa Region; SAR = South Asia Region.

regions are in group A or B). There are only a few good practice examples in the Africa (AFR) and Middle East and North Africa (MNA) Regions (under 25 % of countries). Most AFR and MNA countries have little or no visibility on the web in terms of publishing budget data, and a large proportion are in group C or D.

The EU member states (23 out of 27) and OECD members (31 out of 34) present extensive or significant budget data on the web, but again only a few present evidence on the source and reliability of open budget data (6 in EU, 11 in OECD). Similarly, APEC member economies (18 out of 21 in group A or B) have well-designed publishing sites, but only 7 publish open budget data from FMIS.

The remainder of this chapter provides detailed findings from the data analysis, broken down by country income level, and region, in the following order:

- Existence of dedicated websites for publishing PF data   [I-1, I-2]
- Source and reliability of budget data   [I-3 to I-6]
- Scope and presentation quality of PF information   [I-7 to I-10]
- Contents and regularity of key PF information   [I-11 to I-20]
- Informative indicators   [I-21 to I-40]
- Characteristics of underlying FMIS solutions
- Comparison of findings with Public Expenditure and Financial Accountability (PEFA) indicators
- Comparison with Open Budget Index
- Comparison with other dimensions.

Existence of Dedicated Websites for Publishing Public Finance Data

There are two indicators (I-1 and I-2) under this category, and the responses to relevant questions (derived from Q1 and Q2) are summarized below.

I-1	Is there a dedicated public finance publication website?				
Points	Responses	Economies	%E	Regions	%R
2	There is a dedicated PF website, and links to budget-related publications/reports are clearly visible from the home page.	125	63.1	102	60.7
1	Budget data links are not clearly visible from the home page or posted on separate sites (without a link with home page).	41	20.7	37	22.0
0	There is no dedicated website for publishing PF information.	32	16.2	29	17.3

Taking into account country differences in organizational structures and web practice, the team screened the relevant websites in the following order:

- The Finance Ministry/Department (MoF) websites were screened first, to see if all questions can be answered from one dedicated source.
- In addition to the MoF, Statistics, and Central Bank websites, other ministry/agency web publishing platforms were also visited to capture remaining information not visible in the MoF websites (for example, investment plans, audit reports, procurement).

Most of the governments (166 out of 198, or 83.8 %) have dedicated websites to publish PF data, and for 125 of these (63.1 %), a link to budget data is clearly visible from their home pages. Of the 32 governments (16.2 %) that have no PF website, most are LICs or LMICs (Figure 3.2). Most of the fragile states have dedicated websites (23 out of 35) but the scope of published PF information is limited.

The pattern of Regional distribution is similar. Most of the countries (139 out of 168, or 82.7 %) have dedicated sites to publish PF information, and 102

Figure 3.2 Income level and regional distributions for Indicator 1

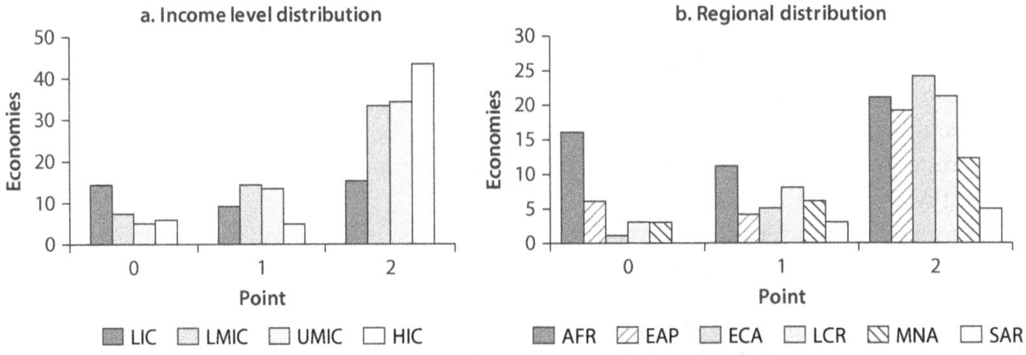

Source: World Bank data.
Note: LIC = Low-Income Country; LMIC = Lower-Middle-Income Country; UMIC = Upper-Middle-Income Country; HIC = High-Income Country. AFR = Africa Region, EAP = East Asia and Pacific Region; ECA = Europe and Central Asia Region; LCR = Latin America and Caribbean Region; MNA = Middle East and North Africa Region; SAR = South Asia Region.

governments (60.7 %) provide easy access to relevant publications. Of the 29 (17.3 %) governments with no PF publication website, most are in AFR.

All EU member states (27), OECD members (34), and APEC member economies (21) have dedicated websites to publish extensive or significant PF information.

I-2	Is there a website/document about the FMIS solution?				
Points	Responses	Economies	%E	Regions	%R
2	There is a specific website presenting the characteristics of FMIS solutions, or the current status of FMIS implementation.	92	46.5	74	44.1
1	There is only published reference document(s) about FMIS implementation.	83	41.9	77	45.8
0	There is no website or document about the FMIS solution.	23	11.6	17	10.1

Nearly half of the governments (92 out of 198, or 46.5 %) have websites that provide useful information about the status of the FMIS and describe the functionality and technology architecture. However, the remaining 106 countries have little or no information about their FMIS: 83 economies publish some reports partially describing FMIS functionality and scope, but there is no information about the FMIS in 23 economies. This pattern characterizes all income levels (see Figure 3.3).

Among the World Bank Regions, 74 countries have dedicated FMIS-related websites. LCR countries are the most informative, in terms of explaining their FMIS through comprehensive information presented in dedicated websites. AFR, ECA, EAP, and SAR follow, with a relatively large group of countries presenting useful information about their FMIS platforms. Most AFR and MNA countries have no information about their FMIS platforms on the web. Only 8 out of 35 fragile states (23 %) have dedicated FMIS websites.

Figure 3.3 Income level and regional distributions for Indicator 2

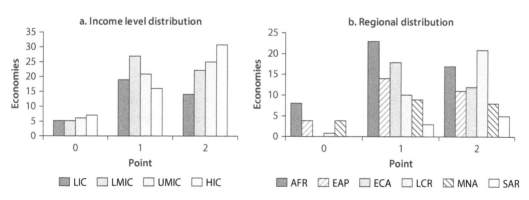

Source: World Bank data.
Note: LIC = Low-Income Country; LMIC = Lower-Middle-Income Country; UMIC = Upper-Middle-Income Country; HIC = High-Income Country. AFR = Africa Region, EAP = East Asia and Pacific Region; ECA = Europe and Central Asia Region; LCR = Latin America and Carribean Region; MNA = Middle East and North Africa Region; SAR = South Asia Region.

Financial Management Information Systems and Open Budget Data
http://dx.doi.org/10.1596/978-1-4648-0083-2

Most of the EU (27) and OECD (34) members, and all APEC economies (21), have dedicated websites or documents describing their FMIS platforms.

Seven HICs have no website for presenting budget data or FMIS platforms, and 11 UMICs/LMICs have little or no visibility on the web.

Source and Reliability of Budget Data

The results obtained from the four indicators in this category (I-3 to I-6) revealed that only a small group of countries present evidence about the source and reliability of the PF data published on their websites. Most of the information is not linked with the 176 FMIS platforms used by the 198 economies, and there is little focus on publishing open budget data (online, free, editable/reusable) from FMIS.

I-3	What is the source of PF data?				
Points	Responses	Economies	%E	Regions	%R
3	Dynamic website (linked with FMIS databases); interactive query options for reports (for example, CSV, XLS, ODF, XML, PDF).	12	6.1	8	4.8
	Argentina; Brazil; Colombia; Finland; Germany; Republic of Korea; Mexico; Peru; Russian Federation; Turkey; United Kingdom; United States				
2	Dynamic website (some linked with databases) to present data from a predefined list of publications (mainly PDF, XLS).	22	11.1	17	10.1
	Bolivia; Chile; China; Denmark; Ecuador; El Salvador; Estonia; Georgia; India; Japan; Kyrgyz Republic; Malta; Netherlands; Nicaragua; Paraguay; Portugal; Singapore; Spain; Sweden; Taiwan, China; Timor-Leste; Ukraine				
1	Static website (not linked to databases) to publish data from unidentified sources (mainly in PDF format).	132	66.7	114	67.9
0	There is no published PF information.	32	16.1	29	17.2

Of the 34 governments that have dynamic websites (user-defined reports generated online), 12 (mostly HICs and UMICs) provide access to rich set of information through interactive queries, mostly linked with FMIS databases. A large number of countries (132 or 66.7 %; mostly HICs and MICs) maintain static websites presenting various documents from unidentified sources (Figure 3.4).

LCR leads in terms of good practices (11 countries with 2 or 3 points), and ECA and EAP follow (6 countries each with 2 or 3 points). Other Regions present PF data mainly through static websites. AFR has the lowest level of visibility in presenting the source of PF data.

Ten EU member states and 15 OECD members have dynamic websites, but most of the developed countries maintain static websites. Similarly, only 10 APEC economies have dynamic PF web publishing sites. Most of the fragile states (21 out of 35) have static websites. Timor-Leste and the Kyrgyz Republic are the only LICs with dynamic websites.

Figure 3.4 Income level and regional distributions for Indicator 3

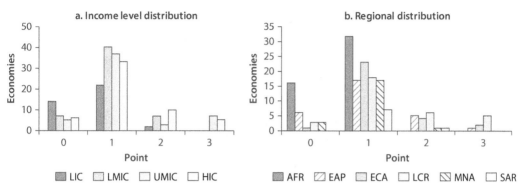

Source: World Bank data.
Note: LIC = Low-Income Country; LMIC = Lower-Middle-Income Country; UMIC = Upper-Middle-Income Country; HIC = High-Income Country. AFR = Africa Region, EAP = East Asia and Pacific Region; ECA = Europe and Central Asia Region; LCR = Latin America and Carribean Region; MNA = Middle East and North Africa Region; SAR = South Asia Region.

I-4	Presence of open budget data (online, editable/reusable, free)				
Points	Responses	Economies	%E	Regions	%R
1	Yes	52	26.3	38	22.6
0	No	146	73.7	130	77.4

Although many governments have FMIS databases and open government initiatives, disclosure of open budget data is not a common practice. To check the extent to which open data are published, the team screened the formats of "public expenditure reports," together with other open data portals publishing budget reports.

Open budget data are visible in 52 economies, but are linked with FMIS databases in only about half (based on the evidence about dynamic websites from I-3). Several LICs and LMICs (13 out of 51) publish open data (Figure 3.5).

Figure 3.5 Income level and regional distributions for Indicator 4

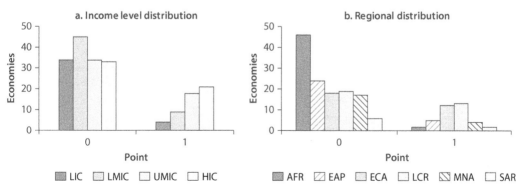

Source: World Bank data.
Note: LIC = Low-Income Country; LMIC = Lower-Middle-Income Country; UMIC = Upper-Middle-Income Country; HIC = High-Income Country. AFR = Africa Region, EAP = East Asia and Pacific Region; ECA = Europe and Central Asia Region; LCR = Latin America and Carribean Region; MNA = Middle East and North Africa Region; SAR = South Asia Region.

LCR and ECA countries lead in publishing open budget data (25 combined), and countries in AFR post the least open budget data. Only 3 of the 35 fragile states can produce some reports using open budget data. Open budget data are visible in less than half of the developed countries (12 EU member states, 19 OECD members, and 10 APEC economies publish open budget data).

I-5	Is system name visible in dynamic/static reports?				
Points	Responses	Economies	%E	Regions	%R
1	Yes	18	9.1	16	9.5
0	No	180	90.9	152	90.5

It is rare to see the name of the underlying FMIS printed as a part of most frequently published "budget execution reports" in static or dynamic websites. Most countries present PF information through PDF files without any indication about the source of data. Only 18 countries include the name of FMIS solution (4 HICs, 8 UMICs, 5 LMICs, 1 LICs) as the source of published information (Figure 3.6).

Among the Regions, relevant good practices are visible in nine LCR countries. Only one fragile state includes the system name in some budget execution reports.

Most of the EU, OECD, and APEC economies do not publish the system name as a part of their regular budget reports (visible only in the reports published by three EU member states, four OECD members, and three APEC economies).

I-6	Is system time stamp visible in dynamic/static reports?				
Points	Responses	Economies	%E	Regions	%R
1	Yes	28	14.1	24	14.3
0	No	170	85.9	144	85.7

Figure 3.6 Income level and regional distributions for Indicator 5

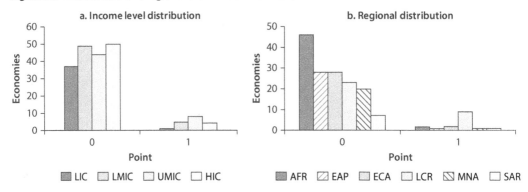

Source: World Bank data.
Note: LIC = Low-Income Country; LMIC = Lower-Middle-Income Country; UMIC = Upper-Middle-Income Country; HIC = High-Income Country. AFR = Africa Region, EAP = East Asia and Pacific Region; ECA = Europe and Central Asia Region; LCR = Latin America and Carribean Region; MNA = Middle East and North Africa Region; SAR = South Asia Region.

Figure 3.7 Income level and regional distributions for Indicator 6

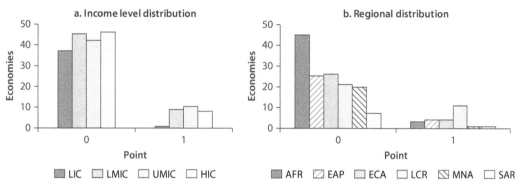

Source: World Bank data.
Note: LIC = Low-Income Country; LMIC = Lower-Middle-Income Country; UMIC = Upper-Middle-Income Country; HIC = High-Income Country. AFR = Africa Region, EAP = East Asia and Pacific Region; ECA = Europe and Central Asia Region; LCR = Latin America and Carribean Region; MNA = Middle East and North Africa Region; SAR = South Asia Region.

The patterns for this indicator are similar to those for system name. Most economies do not print the system date/time from underlying FMIS solutions in frequently published "budget execution reports" or other documents visible on the websites. The 28 countries that do consist of 8 HICs, 10 UMICs, 9 LMICs, and 1 LIC (Figure 3.7).

Again, there are 11 good practice cases in LCR countries, which have a better focus on budget transparency and accountability and a longer history of working with FMIS. Only one fragile state includes the system time in some budget execution reports.

In most of the EU, OECD, and APEC economies the system time stamp is not printed as a part of frequent budget reports (visible only in five EU member states, five OECD members, and eight APEC economies).

Scope and Presentation Quality of Public Finance Information

The scope and presentation quality of PF data published in government websites were analyzed using four indicators (I-7 to I-10) derived from two questions (Q4 and Q5). In this section, it is important to note that the assessment of indicators I-7 and I-8 partially depends on the judgment of reviewers, since it is difficult to quantify quality and scope. These questions were included to gauge the perception of first-time visitors about the presentation of budget data and the level of detail visible at first sight. The other indicators are more specific and were included to complement scope questions.

I-7	Quality: What is the quality of PF data presentation?				
Points	Responses	Economies	%E	Regions	%R
2	Good quality (presented reports are informative and easy to access and read).	69	34.8	50	29.8
1	Partially acceptable (some of the published PF info is useful).	97	49.0	89	53.0
0	Below desired level (most of the published PF info is not informative).	32	16.2	29	17.2

Figure 3.8 Income level and regional distributions for Indicator 7

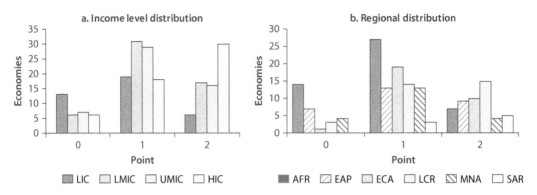

Source: World Bank data.
Note: LIC = Low-Income Country; LMIC = Lower-Middle-Income Country; UMIC = Upper-Middle-Income Country; HIC = High-Income
Country. AFR = Africa Region, EAP = East Asia and Pacific Region; ECA = Europe and Central Asia Region; LCR = Latin America and
Carribean Region; MNA = Middle East and North Africa Region; SAR = South Asia Region.

Of the 69 governments that provide comprehensive information about budget performance in easy-to-understand formats, 30 are HICs, 16 UMICs, 17 LMICs, and 6 LICs. However, the quality of reporting in a large portion of PF websites (49 %) is only partially acceptable. most of the reports are not very informative, or are too detailed, without clear instructions on how to interpret results. There are 32 websites with little or no attention to the quality of the presentation (Figure 3.8).

In the Regions, a relatively small number of PF publishing sites (29.8 %) are well maintained, with regular updates on budget results. LCR stands out with the largest number of good-quality websites (15), followed by ECA (10), EAP (9), and AFR (7). About half of the Regional PF websites present some useful data, but may benefit from substantial improvements; and only 6 fragile states present informative and detailed reports. Most of the EU, OPEC, and APEC members maintain good-quality websites to publish timely budget results.

I-8	Content: Is there sufficient level of detail?				
Points	Responses	Economies	%E	Regions	%R
1	Yes	**148**	74.7 %	**123**	73.2 %
0	No	**50**	25.3 %	**45**	26.8 %

This indicator serves as a rapid assessment of the extent of information published on websites. It is not designed to drill down into published reports and analyze the contents, since other indices (for example, open budget index [OBI], Report on Observance of Standards and Codes [ROSC]) review the contents of key publications. This indicator should be used with caution, since there is always a possibility of missing some of the features that may not be obvious at first glance.

Figure 3.9 Income level and regional distributions for Indicator 8

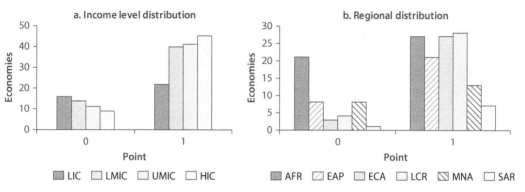

Source: World Bank data.

Note: LIC = Low-Income Country; LMIC = Lower-Middle-Income Country; UMIC = Upper-Middle-Income Country; HIC = High-Income Country. AFR = Africa Region, EAP = East Asia and Pacific Region; ECA = Europe and Central Asia Region; LCR = Latin America and Carribean Region; MNA = Middle East and North Africa Region; SAR = South Asia Region.

A large number of economies provide substantial information on various subjects, but 50 provide minimal or no information about the contents of publications. The level of comprehensiveness increases from LICs to HICs. Almost all of the EU, OECD, and APEC member economies have comprehensive websites providing useful details about the budget performance.

LCR has the highest number of comprehensive websites (28 out of 123), followed by ECA (27), EAP (21), AFR (27), MNA (13), and SAR (7). Many AFR countries (44 %) have inadequate web contents for sharing budget execution results, as do several EAP and MNA countries. More than half of the fragile states have little or no detail about the budget results on their websites (Figure 3.9).

I-9	Are presented budget results easy to understand (Citizens Budget)?				
Points	Responses	Economies	%E	Regions	%R
2	Yes (comprehensive information in meaningful format for the citizens. highly interactive)	15	7.6	12	7.1
1	Yes (basic information about the budget cycle and some results in meaningful format)	33	16.7	26	15.5
0	No (minimal or no information about Citizens Budget)	150	75.7	130	77.4

This indicator measures whether meaningful budget data are accessible online to citizens in a simple and easy-to-understand format. In many countries, such documents/web contents are referred to as the Citizens Budget, and are considered as an important indicator of fiscal transparency. Obviously, the Citizens Budget should be credible and timely, and the source of information should be reliable. This study simply aims to locate such documents or websites for comparative analysis, and to expose the contents; it is beyond the scope of this study to analyze such documents, and the impact of citizen feedback on budget planning, in detail.

Figure 3.10 Income level and regional distributions for Indicator 9

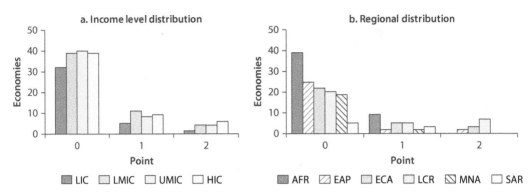

Source: World Bank data.
Note: LIC = Low-Income Country; LMIC = Lower-Middle-Income Country; UMIC = Upper-Middle-Income Country; HIC = High-Income
Country. AFR = Africa Region, EAP = East Asia and Pacific Region; ECA = Europe and Central Asia Region; LCR = Latin America and
Carribean Region; MNA = Middle East and North Africa Region; SAR = South Asia Region.

Only about 15 of the 198 governments provide interactive platforms for citizens' access to meaningful budget data and feedback provision through dedicated Citizens Budget websites. Another 33 present useful information for the citizens on some of the important aspects of budget spending; however, most governments do not provide meaningful information to their citizens on budget results. These observations are valid for all income levels (see Figure 3.10). Of developed countries, only a relatively small number have interactive Citizens Budget websites—about 35–40 % of EU, OECD, and APEC members.

There are about 12 Citizens Budget websites with an easy-to-understand graphical user interface, mainly in LCR and ECA. Other Regions have about 26 useful Citizens Budget websites presenting mainly static information (PDF files describing the budget performance in easy-to-understand format). However, most countries in all Regions, and particularly in AFR, do not have Citizens Budget websites. Only 3 of the 35 fragile states have useful Citizens Budget websites providing limited information.

I-10	Are the details of budget classification/chart of accounts published?				
Points	Responses	Economies	%E	Regions	%R
1	Yes	**93**	47.0	**75**	**44.6**
0	No	**105**	53.0	**93**	55.4

A budget classification (BC) with a sufficiently detailed segment structure is very important for the production of comprehensive and reliable PF data sets. A unified chart of accounts (CoA) is essential for consistently recording transactions and balances (flows and stocks) in the general ledger. BC and CoA are interrelated: it is advisable to design the BC as a subset of the CoA to ensure correspondence between entries recorded in each of these classifications and to

Figure 3.11 Income level and regional distributions for Indicator 10

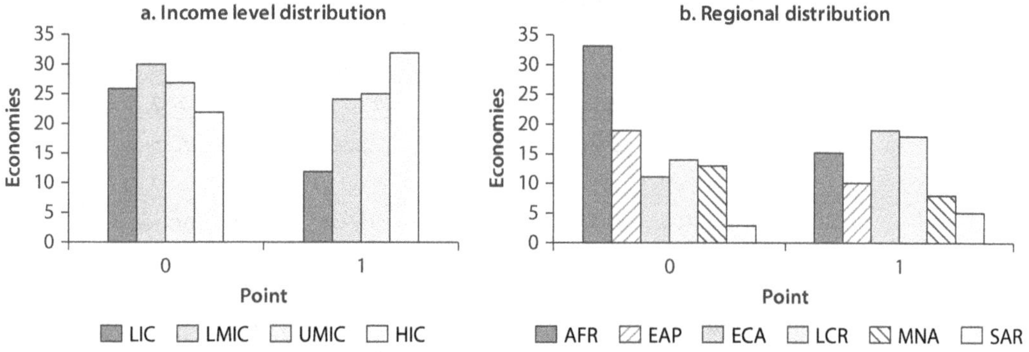

a. Income level distribution

b. Regional distribution

LIC   LMIC   UMIC   HIC   AFR   EAP   ECA   LCR   MNA   SAR

Source: World Bank data.
Note: LIC = Low-Income Country; LMIC = Lower-Middle-Income Country; UMIC = Upper-Middle-Income Country; HIC = High-Income Country. AFR = Africa Region; EAP = East Asia and Pacific Region; ECA = Europe and Central Asia Region; LCR = Latin America and Carribean Region; MNA = Middle East and North Africa Region; SAR = South Asia Region.

properly link budget and treasury accounts. Many countries use the same number of digits and subsegments for CoA and the Economic segment. This indicator was designed to check the level of detail presented for BC and CoA on PF websites, to clarify the key parameters used in recording and reporting PF data.

Of the 198 governments, 93 provide the details of BC/CoA on their websites. About half of the HICs and MICs (50.6 %) publish the data structures (or sometimes a full listing) of their BC/CoA (Figure 3.11), as do many EU members (21 out of 27), OPEC countries (27 out of 34), and APEC economies (14 out of 21).

More than half of the countries in LCR, ECA, and SAR publish the BC/CoA details, but only 34 % of the countries in AFR, EAP, and MNA do so. Of the 35 fragile states, 10 publish the BC/CoA listings on their websites.

These results may indicate that many economies do not pay enough attention to the design (or optimization) of their BC/CoA data structures to be able to capture maximum budget information with minimum number of digits, and to store a large number of transactions historically and retrieve data rapidly.

Contents and Regularity of PF Information

The 10 indicators (I-11 to I-20) in this category, derived from 5 questions (Q6 to Q10), measure the existence of key budget documents and the regularity of publication in selected categories. The frequency and regularity of key budget execution publications (planned/actual figures for all revenues and expenditures) were captured in I-17 and I-18 (Q9). Additionally, several other indicators (I-21 to I-30) were used to collect information about specific sections of public expenditure reports published on the web. Some of these details (for example, sectoral analysis or subnational-level spending) are not published at the same frequency as the major spending reports. It was beyond the scope of this study to analyze or verify in depth the details of PF data in various reports. However, relevant web links are included to provide quick access to specific details for further analysis.

I-11	Approved annual budget published?						
I-12	If yes: Regularity of publishing annual budget plans						

Points	Responses	Economies	%E	Regularity	Regions	%R	Regularity
1	Yes	153	77.3	120	128	76.2	98
0	No	45	22.7	—	40	23.8	—

Most of the HICs and MICs publish their approved annual budgets on the PF websites. About 82 % of the HICs and UMICs follow good practices in terms of the regularity of reporting—that is, publishing without interruption, at least within the last five years (levels are indicated by a line on each bar in Figure 3.12)—and present their approved budgets on the web before the upcoming budget year. Some 120 economies (78.4 %) publish the approved budget regularly, sometimes after the start of the budget year. Almost all EU, OECD, and APEC governments publish their approved annual budgets regularly.

Most of the countries in the Regions (except AFR) publish their approved annual budget plans before the relevant budget year, and about 98 (76 %) of them do so regularly (except in AFR, where only 52 % publish these plans regularly). Of the 35 fragile states, 20 publish their approved budgets, and 13 of them do so regularly.

I-13	Medium-Term Expenditure Framework documents published?						
I-14	If yes: Regularity of publishing MTEF plans						

Points	Responses	Economies	%E	Regularity	Regions	%R	Regularity
1	Yes	103	52.0	64	81	48.2	44
0	No	95	48.0	—	87	51.8	—

Figure 3.12 Income level and regional distributions for Indicators 11 and 12

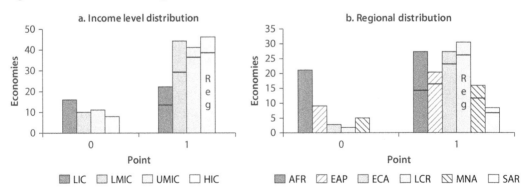

Source: World Bank data.
Note: LIC = Low-Income Country; LMIC = Lower-Middle-Income Country; UMIC = Upper-Middle-Income Country; HIC = High-Income Country. AFR = Africa Region, EAP = East Asia and Pacific Region; ECA = Europe and Central Asia Region; LCR = Latin America and Carribean Region; MNA = Middle East and North Africa Region; SAR = South Asia Region.

Figure 3.13 Income level and regional distributions for Indicators 13 and 14

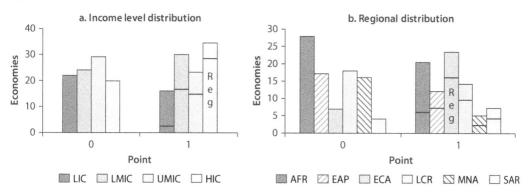

Source: World Bank data.

Note: LIC = Low-Income Country; LMIC = Lower-Middle-Income Country; UMIC = Upper-Middle-Income Country; HIC = High-Income Country. AFR = Africa Region, EAP = East Asia and Pacific Region; ECA = Europe and Central Asia Region; LCR = Latin America and Carribean Region; MNA = Middle East and North Africa Region; SAR = South Asia Region.

About half of the HICs and MICs publish their multiyear plans, or medium-term expenditure framework (MTEF), and 64 regularly update these plans (revising them every year, at least within the last five years). In LMICs and LICs, the regularity of publishing MTEF information is relatively lower (Figure 3.13). About 80 % of the EU, OECD, and APEC economies publish and regularly update their MTEF plans.

About 44 ECA, LCR, and SAR countries publish MTEF data regularly, but regular publication of MTEF data is much less common in AFR, MNA, and EAP countries. Of the 35 fragile states, 10 present some reports on MTEF plans, but most do not do so regularly.

I-15	Public investment plans published?							
I-16	If yes: Regularity of publishing public investment plans							
Points	Responses	Economies	%E	Regularity	Regions	%R	Regularity
1	Yes	**44**	22.2	32	**38**	22.6	27
0	No	**154**	77.8	—	**130**	77.4	—

Only 44 governments publish public investment plans (Figure 3.14). However, in many cases (for example, Ukraine) the public investments are included as a part of the approved annual budgets and listed in MTEF documents; hence this indicator may not accurately capture all public investment plans that are made available. Among these 44 economies, about 60 % of HICs and MICs publish investment plans regularly, as do similar proportions of EU, OECD, and APEC economies.

A relatively small number of Regional governments (mainly in LCR and ECA) publish multiyear investment plans regularly, and most of the Regional countries do not publish their investment plans separately. A large number of

Figure 3.14 Income level and regional distributions for Indicators 15 and 16

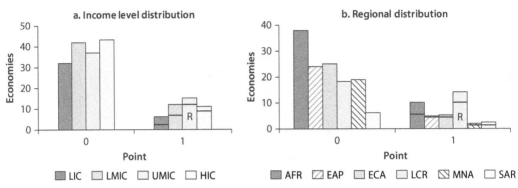

Source: World Bank data.
Note: LIC = Low-Income Country; LMIC = Lower-Middle-Income Country; UMIC = Upper-Middle-Income Country; HIC = High-Income Country. AFR = Africa Region, EAP = East Asia and Pacific Region; ECA = Europe and Central Asia Region; LCR = Latin America and Carribean Region; MNA = Middle East and North Africa Region; SAR = South Asia Region.

countries (except in AFR) present their investments within the approved annual budget plans; the actual level of publishing investment plans is estimated as 50 % in all Regions. Investment plans are published in a few of the fragile states (4 out of 35).

I-17	Budget execution results published?						
I-18	If yes: Regularity of publishing budget execution results						
Points	Responses	Economies	%E	Regularity	Regions	%R	Regularity
1	Yes	**147**	74.2	*117*	**124**	73.8	*96*
0	No	**51**	25.8	—	**44**	26.2	—

Most of the economies (largely HICs and MICs) publish budget execution results at different intervals (Figure 3.15)—monthly in 50 of the 147, quarterly in 18, and annually in the remaining 78. Among these countries, about 80 % publish these results regularly. It appears that only a small group of countries publish budget performance with monthly updates, and a large portion present the results annually. There seems to be room for many countries to make substantial improvements by using their existing FMIS to publish more frequently (monthly).

A large number of the regional governments publish their budget execution results, most regularly. Many countries publish the budget performance reports (comparing plans versus actuals) annually. A small number of governments in LCR, ECA, EAP, and SAR benefit from their FMIS capabilities to publish the status of budget execution monthly. However, most countries in AFR, MNA, and other Regions publish annual results after the completion of the budget year, without any benefit for performance monitoring during the execution period. Therefore, there is a substantial opportunity cost in not disclosing the budget

Figure 3.15 Income level and regional distributions for Indicators 17 and 18

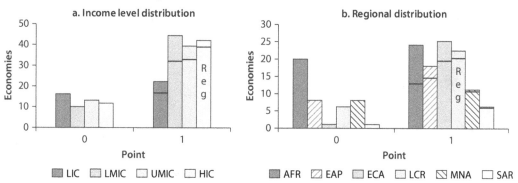

Source: World Bank data.
Note: LIC = Low-Income Country; LMIC = Lower-Middle-Income Country; UMIC = Upper-Middle-Income Country; HIC = High-Income Country. AFR = Africa Region, EAP = East Asia and Pacific Region; ECA = Europe and Central Asia Region; LCR = Latin America and Carribean Region; MNA = Middle East and North Africa Region; SAR = South Asia Region.

reports frequently (monthly). About 50 % of the fragile states follow a similar pattern: 14 of the 35 countries publish this information, mostly annually.

Budget execution results are presented through regular updates in more than 80 % of the EU, OECD, and APEC economies. However, monthly publication of budget performance based on FMIS databases is rare (as was already explained under Indicators I-3 and I-4).

I-19	External audit of central government budget operations published?							
I-20	If yes: Regularity of publishing external audit reports							
Points	Responses	Economies	%E	Regularity	Regions	%R	Regularity
1	Yes	**76**	38.4	61	**59**	35.1	44
0	No	**122**	61.6	—	**109**	64.9	—

This indicator checks whether budget-related audit reports are published on external audit organization websites. In most of the economies, publication of external audit reports is mandated by law. However, such reports are usually submitted to parliaments to comply with the legislation, and it is rare to see them published on the web to inform citizens. Publication of such reports on PF websites could improve budget transparency and accountability in many economies. Hence, there seem to be opportunities to improve current practices.

This study found that 76 governments publish some reports about budget execution performance on external audit websites (usually within 6–12 months after the closing of the budget year), and 61 of them (81 %, mainly HICs and MICs) present such assessments regularly (Figure 3.16). Only 6 of the 38 LIC countries publish external audit reports regularly, and under half of the EU, OECD, and APEC governments do so. In summary, most countries do not pay enough attention to presenting external audit reports regularly on the web.

Figure 3.16 Income level and regional distributions for Indicators 19 and 20

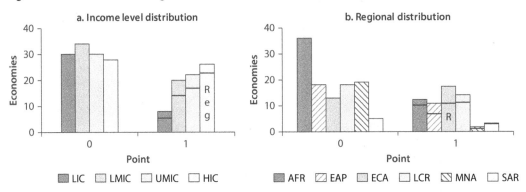

Source: World bank data.
Note: LIC = Low-Income Country; LMIC = Lower-Middle-Income Country; UMIC = Upper-Middle-Income Country; HIC = High-Income Country. AFR = Africa Region, EAP = East Asia and Pacific Region; ECA = Europe and Central Asia Region; LCR = Latin America and Carribean Region; MNA = Middle East and North Africa Region; SAR = South Asia Region.

Among the Regions, a number of countries in LCR, ECA, EAP, and SAR publish external audit reports related to budget execution, but only a few do so within six months after the closing of the budget year. In fragile states only 6 out of 35 countries publish some audit reports, and only 4 of these do so regularly.

Informative Indicators

There are 20 informative indicators (I-21 to I-40) derived from 10 questions (Q11 to Q20) to provide additional feedback about other important features of PF publication websites. Indicators I-21 to I-30 are designed to clarify the contents of budget execution reports by providing additional feedback on several specific report sections that are visible on the PF websites, for further analysis.

I-21	Public expenditures > Consolidated budget results published?				
Points	Responses	Economies	%E	Regions	%R
1	Yes	**140**	70.7	**116**	69.0
0	No	**58**	29.3	**52**	31.0

Most of the governments (mainly HICs and MICs) publish consolidated budget results at different intervals (Figure 3.17). Almost all EU, OECD, and APEC members present consolidate budget results more frequently (monthly/quarterly).

Of the 168 Regional countries, 116 (most in LCR, ECA, SAR, and EAP) publish consolidated results during the budget execution cycle. Also, 16 of the 35 fragile states present the consolidated budget results with annual updates.

Figure 3.17 Income level and regional distributions for Indicator 21

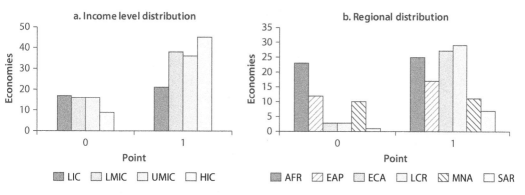

Source: World bank data
Note: LIC = Low-Income Country; LMIC = Lower-Middle-Income Country; UMIC = Upper-Middle-Income Country; HIC = High-Income
Country. AFR = Africa Region, EAP = East Asia and Pacific Region; ECA = Europe and Central Asia Region; LCR = Latin America and
Carribean Region; MNA = Middle East and North Africa Region; SAR = South Asia Region.

Figure 3.18 Income level and regional distributions for Indicator 22

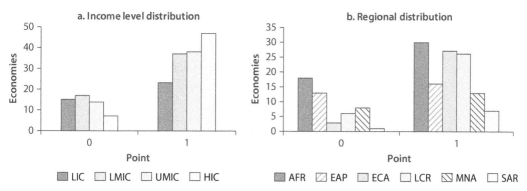

Source: World Bank data.
Note: LIC = Low-Income Country; LMIC = Lower-Middle-Income Country; UMIC = Upper-Middle-Income Country; HIC = High-Income
Country. AFR = Africa Region, EAP = East Asia and Pacific Region; ECA = Europe and Central Asia Region; LCR = Latin America and
Carribean Region; MNA = Middle East and North Africa Region; SAR = South Asia Region.

I-22	Public expenditures > Sector analysis published?				
Points	Responses	Economies	%E	Regions	%R
1	Yes	**145**	73.2	**119**	70.8
0	No	**53**	26.8	**49**	29.2

Sector analysis is important for monitoring the effectiveness of spending in
priority areas. FMIS can be linked with other databases to present comprehensive
information for better forecasting and decision support, by adding specific
dimensions to budget data. It appears that such analytical processing platforms
are rare in the public sector.

Most of the governments (mainly HICs and MICs) publish an analysis of
spending by sectors (Figure 3.18). Comprehensive sector analysis is available in
a large number of the budget execution reports published by the EU, OECD, and

APEC economies, as well. However, many of these reports are published annually, as a part of budget reviews, and in only a few cases is sectoral analysis provided during the execution period.

In the Regions 119 countries publish sector analysis. LCR, ECA, SAR, and AFR countries lead in publishing sector analysis (mainly focused on the education, health, energy, and transport sectors). Finally, 19 of the 35 fragile states publish sector analysis as part of their annual budget performance assessments.

I-23	Public expenditures > Regional analysis published?				
Points	Responses	Economies	%E	Regions	%R
1	Yes	**58**	29.3	**47**	28.0
0	No	**138**	69.7	**119**	70.8
—	n/a	**2**	1.0	**2**	1.2

Information about the regional analysis of spending is important for the assessment of budget performance at state/province/district levels. When linked with FMIS databases, regional spending patterns can be monitored dynamically (through monthly updates) to improve public finance management (PFM) practices. Few published budget execution reports focus on such aspects.

Some of the HICs and MICs publish a regional analysis of spending and present the results through geomapping as well. However, there is little attention to regional analysis in LICs (Figure 3.19). About half of the EU, OECD, and APEC governments regularly publish regional spending analysis.

Of the 47 Regional countries that publish regional analysis, 41 are in ECA, LCR, EAP, and AFR; countries in the other Regions present little information about regional spending patterns on the web. Only 7 of the 35 fragile states present some reports on regional spending.

Figure 3.19 Income level and regional distributions for Indicator 23

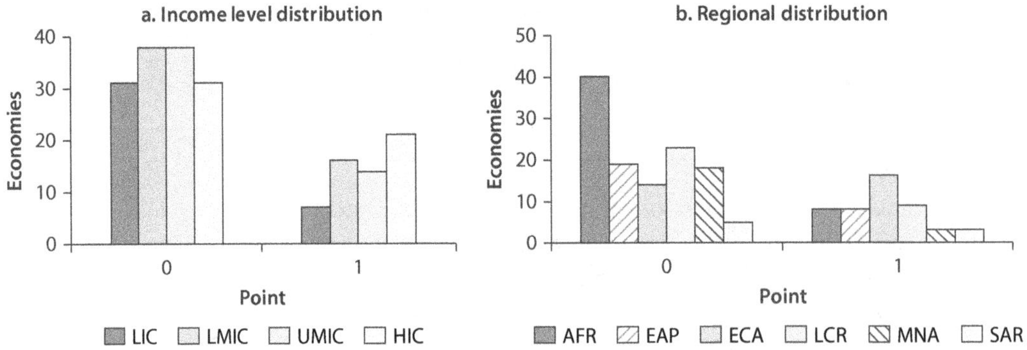

Source: World Bank data.
Note: LIC = Low-Income Country; LMIC = Lower-Middle-Income Country; UMIC = Upper-Middle-Income Country; HIC = High-Income Country. AFR = Africa Region, EAP = East Asia and Pacific Region; ECA = Europe and Central Asia Region; LCR = Latin America and Carribean Region; MNA = Middle East and North Africa Region; SAR = South Asia Region.

Figure 3.20 Income level and regional distributions for Indicator 24

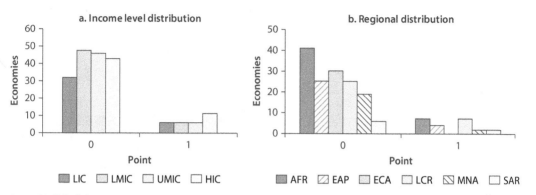

Source: World Bank data.

Note: LIC = Low-Income Country; LMIC = Lower-Middle-Income Country; UMIC = Upper-Middle-Income Country; HIC = High-Income Country. AFR = Africa Region, EAP = East Asia and Pacific Region; ECA = Europe and Central Asia Region; LCR = Latin America and Carribean Region; MNA = Middle East and North Africa Region; SAR = South Asia Region.

I-24	Public expenditures > Gender analysis published?				
Points	Responses	Economies	%E	Regions	%R
1	Yes	**29**	14.6	**22**	13.1
0	No	**169**	85.4	**146**	86.9

Gender analysis is included in expenditure reports published by 29 governments (Figure 3.20), but most of the annual budgets do not include a specific "gender budget" section. Similarly, only some EU, OECD, and APEC governments publish reports with a gender focus.

Except for 18 LCR, AFR, and EAP countries, most Regional countries do not present gender analysis in their budget execution reports (published mostly annually). Only 5 fragile states publish some information related to gender analysis.

I-25	Public expenditures > Analysis of spending for children and youth published?				
Points	Responses	Economies	%E	Regions	%R
1	Yes	**24**	12.1 %	**19**	11.3 %
0	No	**174**	87.9 %	**149**	88.7 %

Analysis of public spending on children and youth is included in the reports published by 24 governments (Figure 3.21), but most of the annual budgets do not include a specific section dedicated to children. Similarly, only a few EU, OECD, and APEC economies publish reports with a focus on children.

Of the 19 Regional countries that publish specific expenditures for various needs of children and youth, 14 are in AFR, LCR, and EAP; most Regional countries do not publish such information. Only 3 of the 35 fragile states present some data on spending for children/youth.

Figure 3.21 Income level and regional distributions for Indicator 25

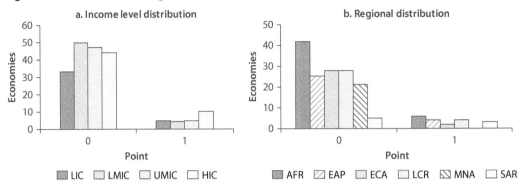

Source: World Bank data.
Note: LIC = Low-Income Country; LMIC = Lower-Middle-Income Country; UMIC = Upper-Middle-Income Country; HIC = High-Income Country. AFR = Africa Region, EAP = East Asia and Pacific Region; ECA = Europe and Central Asia Region; LCR = Latin America and Carribean Region; MNA = Middle East and North Africa Region; SAR = South Asia Region.

Figure 3.22 Income level and regional distributions for Indicator 26

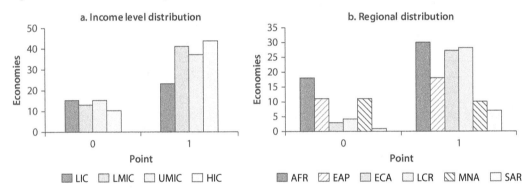

Source: World Bank data.
Note: LIC = Low-Income Country; LMIC = Lower-Middle-Income Country; UMIC = Upper-Middle-Income Country; HIC = High-Income Country. AFR = Africa Region, EAP = East Asia and Pacific Region; ECA = Europe and Central Asia Region; LCR = Latin America and Carribean Region; MNA = Middle East and North Africa Region; SAR = South Asia Region.

I-26	Public expenditures > Debt data published?				
Points	Responses	Economies	%E	Regions	%R
1	Yes	**145**	73.2	**120**	71.4
0	No	**53**	26.8	**48**	28.6

Because of the reporting requirements of lenders, most LICs and MICs tend to publish some data on their foreign debt, but information about domestic or sovereign debt is less visible. A large number of governments publish information about their domestic and/or foreign debt (Figure 3.22). Of these, HICs and MICs (122) publish comprehensive information, usually annually. Also, about 60 % of the LICs publish debt data on their websites. Almost all EU, OECD, and APEC economies publish their domestic/foreign debt data on the PF websites.

Financial Management Information Systems and Open Budget Data
http://dx.doi.org/10.1596/978-1-4648-0083-2

Most of the Regional countries publish significant information about their debt. A large number of AFR, LCR, and ECA countries publish debt data, mostly annually; and 20 of the 35 fragile states also publish data about their foreign/domestic debt.

I-27	Public expenditures > Foreign aid/grants published?				
Points	Responses	Economies	%E	Regions	%R
1	Yes	**123**	62.1	**105**	62.5
0	No	**73**	36.9	**62**	36.9
—	n/a	**2**	1.0	**1**	0.6

Development partners and donors providing foreign aid/grants require regular (quarterly/annual) reporting on the use of funds, mainly from the LICs and LMICs. Donors also have obligations to present information about the funds they provide to various countries for budget support or PFM reforms (investments, advisory support, and capacity building). Despite these requirements, most of the economies do not publish comprehensive information about the use of aid/grant funds on their websites.

Foreign aid/grant details are included in the public expenditure reports of 123 of the 198 economies (Figure 3.23). Half of the LICs (19 out of 38) publish foreign aid data on their websites. A large number of EU, OECD, and APEC economies (around 75 %) publish on the web the aid/grants they provide to developing countries.

In all Regions, 105 countries publish significant aid/grant data, and about half of the fragile states publish information about the aid/grants they receive.

Figure 3.23 Income level and regional distributions for Indicator 27

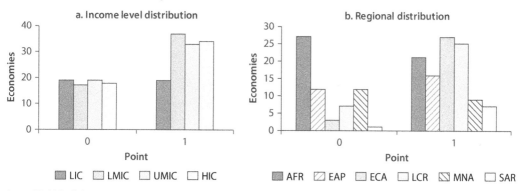

Source: World Bank data.
Note: LIC = Low-Income Country; LMIC = Lower-Middle-Income Country; UMIC = Upper-Middle-Income Country; HIC = High-Income Country. AFR = Africa Region, EAP = East Asia and Pacific Region; ECA = Europe and Central Asia Region; LCR = Latin America and Carribean Region; MNA = Middle East and North Africa Region; SAR = South Asia Region.

I-28	Public expenditures > Fiscal data on state/local governments published?				
Points	Responses	Economies	%E	Regions	%R
1	Yes	**75**	37.9	**59**	35.1
0	No	**121**	61.1	**107**	63.7
—	n/a	**2**	1.0	**2**	1.2

Regular web publication of PF data on state/local level government spending as a part of budget expenditure reports is not a common practice (Figure 3.24). Of the 198 economies, 75 (mainly HICs and MICs) publish significant information (quarterly/annually) about the distribution of revenues and expenditures, with some focus on sectoral spending. However, a large number of economies do not include such details in their web publications. Of EU, OECD, and APEC economies, about 70 % publish such data.

Among regional countries, 59 (35.1 %) publish data about subnational spending. About half of the LCR and ECA countries provide significant data (some with geomapping). AFR has the lowest level of visibility in this regard. Six of the 35 fragile states publish some information about subnational spending.

I-29	Public expenditures > Financial statements published?				
Points	Responses	Economies	%E	Regions	%R
1	Yes	**106**	53.5	**85**	50.6
0	No	**92**	46.5	**83**	49.4

Government financial statements (income statement, balance sheet, and cash flow statement) include the flows and stocks associated with budget operations. The IMF's GFSM 2001 and the International Public Sector Accounting Standards (IPSAS) call for the inclusion of detailed balance sheets reporting the value of

Figure 3.24 Income level and regional distributions for Indicator 28

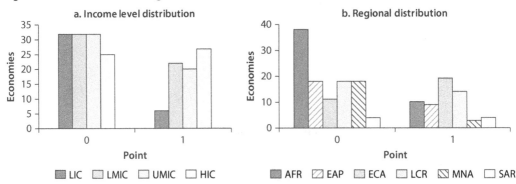

Source: World Bank data.
Note: LIC = Low-Income Country; LMIC = Lower-Middle-Income Country; UMIC = Upper-Middle-Income Country; HIC = High-Income Country. AFR = Africa Region, EAP = East Asia and Pacific Region; ECA = Europe and Central Asia Region; LCR = Latin America and Carribean Region; MNA = Middle East and North Africa Region; SAR = South Asia Region.

Figure 3.25 Income level and regional distributions for Indicator 29

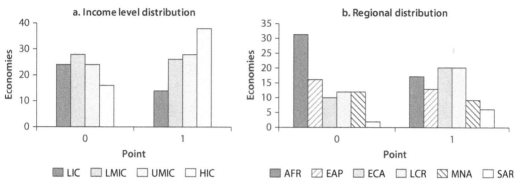

Source: World Bank data.
Note: LIC = Low-Income Country; LMIC = Lower-Middle-Income Country; UMIC = Upper-Middle-Income Country; HIC = High-Income Country. AFR = Africa Region, EAP = East Asia and Pacific Region; ECA = Europe and Central Asia Region; LCR = Latin America and Carribean Region; MNA = Middle East and North Africa Region; SAR = South Asia Region.

financial and nonfinancial assets and liabilities. However, in many countries the data provided in such financial statements are much less than required.

Most of the HICs publish their financial statements regularly, but many MICs and LICs do not. Overall, 106 of the 198 governments publish their financial statements on the web (Figure 3.25). Most of the EU, OECD, and APEC economies (85 %) publish significant information regularly.

Considering all Regions, 85 of the 168 countries present audited financial statements on the web. Larger economies in LCR, ECA, AFR, SAR, and EAP publish significant information related to financial statements. However, many AFR and MNA governments provide little or no information in this regard. Among 35 fragile states, 11 provide some information on their financial statements.

I-30	Public expenditures > Public procurement and contracts published?				
Points	Responses	Economies	%E	Regions	%R
1	Yes	53	26.8 %	41	24.4 %
0	No	145	73.2 %	127	75.6 %

Only a small number of governments (most HICs) follow good practices by publishing comprehensive information about public tenders and execution of contracts signed on dedicated websites/portals (Figure 3.26). Even among EU, OECD, and APEC economies, fewer than 50 % publish significant information on tenders and contracts signed.

Except for several countries in LCR, ECA, and EAP, most Regional governments do not provide comprehensive information about procurement activities. Among fragile states, 5 out of 35 provide some information about tenders.

Figure 3.26 Income level and regional distributions for Indicator 30

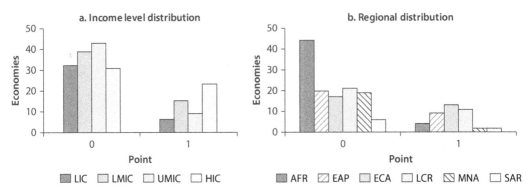

Source: World bank data
Note: LIC = Low-Income Country; LMIC = Lower-Middle-Income Country; UMIC = Upper-Middle-Income Country; HIC = High-Income
Country. AFR = Africa Region, EAP = East Asia and Pacific Region; ECA = Europe and Central Asia Region; LCR = Latin America and
Carribean Region; MNA = Middle East and North Africa Region; SAR = South Asia Region.

Figure 3.27 Income level and regional distributions for Indicator 31

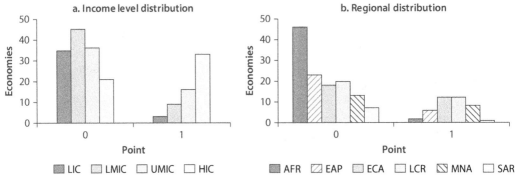

Source: World Bank data.
Note: LIC = Low-Income Country; LMIC = Lower-Middle-Income Country; UMIC = Upper-Middle-Income Country; HIC = High-Income
Country. AFR = Africa Region, EAP = East Asia and Pacific Region; ECA = Europe and Central Asia Region; LCR = Latin America and
Carribean Region; MNA = Middle East and North Africa Region; SAR = South Asia Region.

I-31	Is there an open government/open data website?				
Points	Responses	Economies	%E	Regions	%R
1	Yes	**61**	30.8	**41**	24.4
0	No	**137**	69.2	**127**	75.6

This indicator is designed to capture the web links to country-specific open government/open data initiatives launched as a part of the Open Government Partnership (OGP) or separately. Such websites are visible in 61 economies (Figure 3.27), and interest in launching new open government/open budget websites seems to have grown since 2011.

A large number of HICs and UMICs (49 out of 106) have open data websites with significant data on various aspects (e-Services, access to information, and so on). Only 12 of 92 LICs and LMICs have launched such portals. More than 80 % of EU, OECD, and APEC economies have open government web portals.

Among Regional countries, 24 of the 62 in ECA and LCR maintain useful open government web portals; a total of 41 open government/open data portals are visible in the Regions. Only 1 of the 35 fragile states provides useful information through open government websites.

I-32	Does the FMIS support the PFM needs of state/local governments?				
Points	Responses	Economies	%E	Regions	%R
2	Yes (centralized FMIS solution supports the decentralized SNG automation, data collection, and reporting needs)	16	8.1	15	8.9
1	Yes (FMIS solution provides data collection and consolidation capabilities for the SNGs)	10	5.0	10	6.0
0	No	170	85.9	141	83.9
—	n.a	2	1.0	2	1.2

This indicator is designed to capture evidence about the support provided by centralized web-based FMIS applications to decentralized budget operations at subnational levels. Only a small number of governments (26, or 13.1 %) provide FMIS-based solutions to support state/local budget users (Figure 3.28).

In most of the economies, state- and local-level budget users rely on their own automation solutions for their PFM needs or operate manually (85.9 %). Of the 16 economies that have countrywide FMIS supporting subnational levels, 14 are HICs and MICs. However, the functional scope of such FMIS support is limited to the submission of payment requests, production of budget reports, and consolidation of results. Among EU, OECD, and APEC economies, only some support such subnational operations, mainly because of the decentralized nature of PFM practices.

Figure 3.28 Income level and regional distributions for Indicator 32

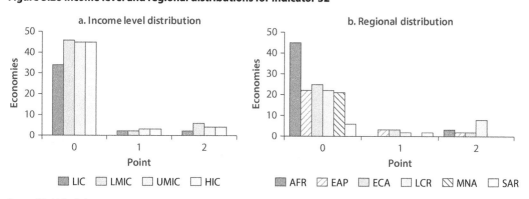

Source: World Bank data.
Note: LIC = Low-Income Country; LMIC = Lower-Middle-Income Country; UMIC = Upper-Middle-Income Country; HIC = High-Income Country. AFR = Africa Region, EAP = East Asia and Pacific Region; ECA = Europe and Central Asia Region; LCR = Latin America and Carribean Region; MNA = Middle East and North Africa Region; SAR = South Asia Region.

Among the Regions, LCR countries are responsible for over half of the good practices (8 out of 15). Among the fragile states, only Afghanistan runs a centralized FMIS solution providing some support for local budget users as well.

I-33	Is there a harmonized public accounting system for all budget levels?				
Points	Responses	Economies	%E	Regions	%R
1	Yes	65	32.8	55	32.7
0	No	131	66.2	111	66.1
—	n.a.	2	1.0	2	1.2

One of the main objectives in many FMIS applications is the production of timely and comprehensive budget reports based on a unified CoA supporting all budget levels. This indicator is designed to locate the websites that provide evidence on a unified CoA and harmonized accounting practices. About 65 governments (mainly HICs and MICs) present documents about the unified CoA and harmonized accounting in central and state/local budget levels (Figure 3.29). About 65 % of the EU, OECD, and APEC economies follow good practices, benefiting from decentralized solutions and consolidating the results through a centralized FMIS.

Among the Regional countries, 55 (mainly from ECA, LCR, and AFR) have harmonized accounting practices and the unified CoA to improve the consolidation and monitoring of budget results. Among the fragile states, 6 benefit from harmonized accounting practices. In summary, a large number of countries continue to run daily PFM operations without a unified CoA and harmonized accounting practices. Centralized FMIS solutions and changes in legal/operational frameworks could bring substantial benefits in terms of operational efficiency and cost savings, especially in LICs and LMICs.

Figure 3.29 Income level and regional distributions for Indicator 33

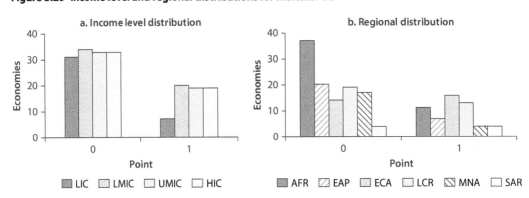

Source: World Bank data.
Note: LIC = Low-Income Country; LMIC = Lower-Middle-Income Country; UMIC = Upper-Middle-Income Country; HIC = High-Income Country. AFR = Africa Region, EAP = East Asia and Pacific Region; ECA = Europe and Central Asia Region; LCR = Latin America and Carribean Region; MNA = Middle East and North Africa Region; SAR = South Asia Region.

| I-34 | Are PF data published on the Statistics website? Or another website? |

Points	Responses	Economies	%E	Regions	%R
3	Both Statistics and other websites publish PF data.	23	11.6	16	9.5
2	Other website publishes PF data (no Statistics website publishes PF data).	36	18.2	31	18.5
1	Statistics website publishes PF data.	39	19.7	30	17.9
0	Statistics website with no PF data.	100	50.5	91	54.1

This indicator is developed to capture other websites (Statistics, Central Bank, or other) on which PF information may be published. In about half of the countries, Statistics Organization websites provide useful information about national accounts (public+private sector results) without a separate section on public finance. A number of countries (39) present additional PF data on their Statistics websites, in addition to their main budget publication websites. Additional budget reports are visible on other government websites in 36 economies where Statistics websites do not contain PF data. Finally, 23 countries provide comprehensive PF data on both Statistics and other websites. The EU, OECD, and APEC economies display similar patterns.

Regional trends are very similar to income level distributions (Figure 3.30). Of the 35 fragile states, 3 provide PF data on other public websites.

| I-35 | Access to information explained? |

Points	Responses	Economies	%E	Regions	%R
1	Yes	53	26.8	34	20.2
0	No	145	73.2	134	79.8

Figure 3.30 Income level and regional distributions for Indicator 34

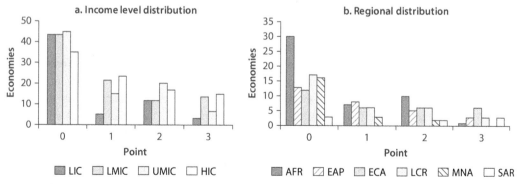

Source: World Bank data.
Note: LIC = Low-Income Country; LMIC = Lower-Middle-Income Country; UMIC = Upper-Middle-Income Country; HIC = High-Income Country. AFR = Africa Region, EAP = East Asia and Pacific Region; ECA = Europe and Central Asia Region; LCR = Latin America and Carribean Region; MNA = Middle East and North Africa Region; SAR = South Asia Region.

Financial Management Information Systems and Open Budget Data
http://dx.doi.org/10.1596/978-1-4648-0083-2

Figure 3.31 Income level and regional distributions for Indicator 35

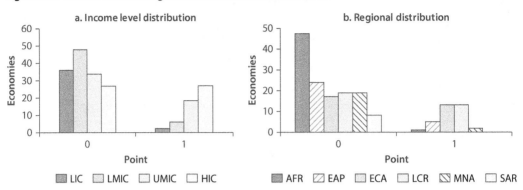

Source: World Bank data.
Note: LIC = Low-Income Country; LMIC = Lower-Middle-Income Country; UMIC = Upper-Middle-Income Country; HIC = High-Income
Country. AFR = Africa Region, EAP = East Asia and Pacific Region; ECA = Europe and Central Asia Region; LCR = Latin America and
Carribean Region; MNA = Middle East and North Africa Region; SAR = South Asia Region.

Most countries provide little explanation of their policies on access to public information. Among the 198 countries screened, only 53 economies (mainly HICs and UMICs) have dedicated websites presenting the details of their access to information policy or documents (Figure 3.31). Practices in publishing relevant information appear to be better in the EU (65 %), OECD (70 %), and APEC (52 %) economies.

Among Regional countries, only 34 publish relevant information. Some of the LCR, ECA, and EAP countries (31 of the 34) follow good practices by providing various options for access to information. No fragile state has a relevant website.

I-36	Are PFM roles and responsibilities clearly explained?				
Points	Responses	Economies	%E	Regions	%R
1	Yes	**143**	72.2 %	**117**	69.6 %
0	No	**55**	27.8 %	**51**	30.4 %

Most of the websites provide useful information about roles and responsibilities in the PFM domain (usually under the home page of PF organizations). About 143 economies explain the PFM roles and organizational structure on their dedicated PF publication websites (Figure 3.32). All EU, OECD, and APEC economies have comprehensive information in this regard, as well.

In the Regions, 117 countries (69.6 %) provide useful information about the organizational structure and PFM roles. The visibility of such clarifications is less in AFR (about 52 % of countries). Among the 35 fragile states, 16 present useful information about PFM roles.

Figure 3.32 Income level and regional distributions for Indicator 36

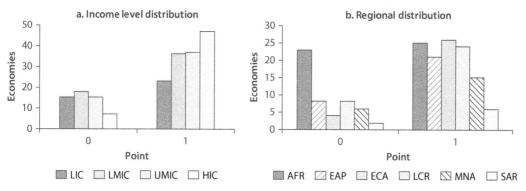

Source: World Bank data.
Note: LIC = Low-Income Country; LMIC = Lower-Middle-Income Country; UMIC = Upper-Middle-Income Country; HIC = High-Income Country. AFR = Africa Region, EAP = East Asia and Pacific Region; ECA = Europe and Central Asia Region; LCR = Latin America and Carribean Region; MNA = Middle East and North Africa Region; SAR = South Asia Region.

I-37	Compliance with specific international reporting standards?				
Points	Responses	Economies	%E	Regions	%R
2	IMF GFS reports are published (including UN COFOG-based functional classification of expenditures).	54	27.3	44	26.2
1	Expenditure reports according to UN COFOG functional classification.	9	4.5	7	4.2
0	Budget reports compliant with national standards only.	135	68.2	117	69.6

This indicator monitors the publication of specific reports (IMF's Government Finance Statistics and UN's COFOG) on PF websites. Most of the governments publish budget reports in line with country-specific reporting standards (Figure 3.33). Internationally accepted reports are published on the dedicated PF websites of 54 economies, of which 36 are HICs and UMICs. There is 40 % GFS and COFOG compliance among EU, OECD, and APEC economies.

Figure 3.33 Income level and regional distributions for Indicator 37

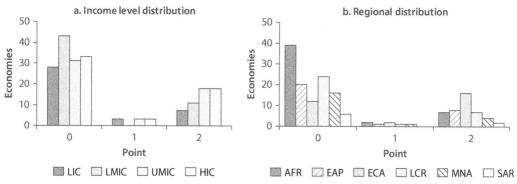

Source: World Bank data.
Note: LIC = Low-Income Country; LMIC = Lower-Middle-Income Country; UMIC = Upper-Middle-Income Country; HIC = High-Income Country. AFR = Africa Region, EAP = East Asia and Pacific Region; ECA = Europe and Central Asia Region; LCR = Latin America and Carribean Region; MNA = Middle East and North Africa Region; SAR = South Asia Region.

Financial Management Information Systems and Open Budget Data
http://dx.doi.org/10.1596/978-1-4648-0083-2

Of the 44 Regional countries that are GFS- and/or COFOG-compliant, 16 are in ECA. Of the 35 fragile states, only 6 publish GFS- and/or COFOG-compliant reports on the web.

I-38	Web statistics (reports on website traffic)?				
Points	Responses	Economies	%E	Regions	%R
1	Yes	29	14.6	23	13.7
0	No	169	85.4	145	86.3

There are a few good practices in providing feedback on website traffic (number of visitors, most frequently visited web pages, and so on). It is difficult to locate such tools, since most of them are managed internally by public entities and the statistics are not shared. However, several countries disclose such statistics (Figure 3.34).

I-39	Which platforms are available for feedback provision?				
Points	Responses	Economies	%E	Regions	%R
3	A number of feedback options are visible (telephone/chat/fax/mail/e-mail/forms/web statistics).	100	50.5	81	48.2
2	Interactive feedback options are visible (telephone/chat/fax/mail).	28	14.2	23	13.7
1	Static feedback options are available (e-mail/feedback forms/web stats).	45	22.7	41	24.4
0	Not visible or inadequate.	25	12.6	23	13.7

A large number of governments (mainly HICs and MICs) provide several options for providing feedback (Figure 3.35). Most of the ECA, LCR, EAP, and SAR countries follow good practices.

Figure 3.34 Income level and regional distributions for Indicator 38

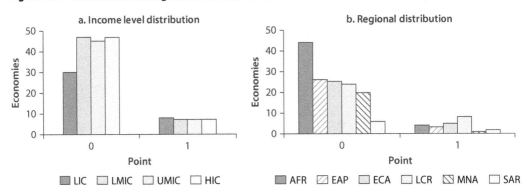

Source: World Bank data.
Note: LIC = Low-Income Country; LMIC = Lower-Middle-Income Country; UMIC = Upper-Middle-Income Country; HIC = High-Income Country. AFR = Africa Region, EAP = East Asia and Pacific Region; ECA = Europe and Central Asia Region; LCR = Latin America and Carribean Region; MNA = Middle East and North Africa Region; SAR = South Asia Region.

Figure 3.35 Income level and regional distributions for Indicator 39

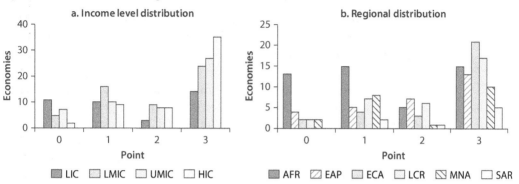

Source: World Bank data.

Note: LIC = Low-Income Country; LMIC = Lower-Middle-Income Country; UMIC = Upper-Middle-Income Country; HIC = High-Income Country. AFR = Africa Region, EAP = East Asia and Pacific Region; ECA = Europe and Central Asia Region; LCR = Latin America and Carribean Region; MNA = Middle East and North Africa Region; SAR = South Asia Region.

I-40   What languages are used to publish PF information?

A majority of the PF web publishing sites are easy to navigate because of the availability of native and other language options. Using online machine translation tools (for example, Google Translate), it was possible to obtain responses to most of the questions while screening the websites. Table 3.2 lists the various language options available in PF websites.

Most of the PF publication websites are accessible in English (54 native, 101 other). Although 109 economies present their PF information in at least one other language, most of the second language options (103) provide substantially reduced information, and key budget reports are presented only in the native language (except in Canada, Malta, and Poland, where publications in another language are comprehensive). Some countries publish their results in a third language (28 out of 198), with reduced scope.

Table 3.2 Indicator 40 > Distribution of native and other language options

Language	Code	Native	Second	Third	All
English	eng	54	82	19	155
French	fre	23	8	—	31
Spanish	spa	21	—	—	21
Arabic	ara	18	3	—	21
Russian	rus	3	6	1	10
Portuguese	por	7	1	1	9
Chinese	chi	4	—	—	4
German	ger	4	—	1	5
Dutch	dut	3	—	—	3
Other	—	61	9	6	76
Totals		**198**	*109*	*28*	*335*

Source: World Bank data.

Characteristics of Underlying FMIS Solutions

The FMIS & OBD data set includes the important characteristics of 176 FMIS platforms that are visible on the web (see Appendix B.2 for the description of related fields). An existing FMIS database that includes the details of 109 FMIS projects funded by the World Bank Group (71 completed + 30 active + 8 pipeline; updated every six months) from 60 countries was used to extract and reuse relevant fields consistently. The team visited the other country websites that were not included in this database to collect additional data and capture the status of all 176 FMIS. The results of this expanded FMIS survey are presented in several groups below to clarify the key features of FMIS platforms that can be used as the basis for open budget data in many countries. This data set is also the basis for the FMIS World Map.

In addition to the web links provided for access to the descriptions of the 176 FMIS, the new data set includes the full name and abbreviation of all operational systems. There seems to be no naming convention that is shared by a number of countries to define different types of FMIS based on their scope, functionality, technology architecture, or application software platforms. Many countries prefer to give their systems unique names, and several regional patterns have emerged over the years, mainly in LCR, ECA, and AFR. The name *Integrated FMIS (IFMIS)* or its different language versions is popular in many countries, despite the fact that the term refers mainly to core FMIS solutions, and does not include a data warehouse for full integration with other PFM systems to publish reliable open budget data. As was explained in chapter 1, IFMIS solutions are rare in practice, and using the term as a synonym for core FMIS functionality may be misleading.

Regarding the PFM topology, 166 of the 198 economies (83.8 %) operate a centralized FMIS solution to support decentralized operations at various budget levels (Figure 3.36). The remaining 32 economies (16.2 %) have distributed FMIS solutions that are managed by executive line ministries, and a centralized system is used to consolidate data from distributed databases.

According to the description of the systems in PF websites, most of the FMIS solutions that are operational in 120 countries (68.2 %) support the budget preparation, execution, accounting, and financial reporting functions (B+T) as core capabilities (Figure 3.37), and some of them have additional modules

Figure 3.36 PFM topology supported by FMIS solutions

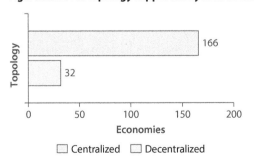

Figure 3.37 Functionality of FMIS solutions

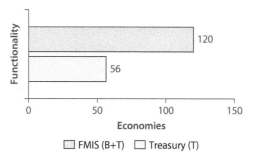

Source: World Bank data.
Note: PFM = Public Finance Management; FMIS =
Financial Management Information System.

Figure 3.38 Operational status of FMIS solutions

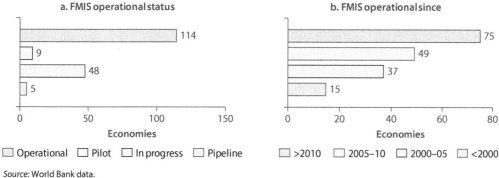

Source: World Bank data.
Note: FMIS = Financial Management Information System.

(human resources management information system/payroll, procurement, asset management, and so on). The other 56 solutions (31.8 %) provide core budget execution, accounting, and reporting capabilities only, and are usually referred to as Treasury Systems (T).

The team used existing websites and the reference documents posted on the web to check the operational status of FMIS platforms (Figure 3.38). The initial findings were later verified by some of the government officials, and the data set was updated accordingly. The results indicate that 114 of the 176 FMIS solutions (64.8 %) are used to support PFM functions on a daily basis, and there are 9 pilot implementations that are partially operational. It appears that 48 economies are in the middle of modernization projects to improve their FMIS, and there are 5 pipeline projects to implement new solutions. Most of the existing systems (123 of the 176, or 70 %) have been operational since 2005, and they benefit from relatively new web-based platforms that are designed to improve operational efficiency and provide timely decision support.

In 106 economies (60 %), FMIS support both central- and local-level budget operations (C+L) of executive ministries (mainly the Finance Ministry or Department) through web-based systems. The FMIS platforms in the 70

Figure 3.39 Scope of FMIS solutions

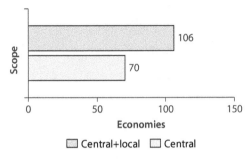

Source: World Bank data.
Note: FMIS = Financial Management Information System.

Figure 3.40 FMIS application software solutions

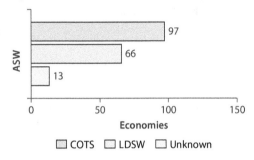

remaining countries are designed to support mainly central budget operations (C) for the line ministries, and various public entities at state/local budget levels run distributed systems for their needs (Figure 3.39).

In addition, a large group of economies (97 of 176, or 55.1 %) have developed FMIS solutions based on commercial off-the-shelf (COTS) packages, customized for public sector needs (Figure 3.40). About 66 economies (37.5 %) have invested considerable time and effort to develop and maintain locally developed software (LDSW) solutions, mainly to have full access to the source code and databases and reduce the costs of licensing and support. The type of application software is unknown in 13 economies (7.4 %), since most of these countries either do not publish such details on the web or operate manually.

Because of the advances in technology and the rapid expansion of the World Wide Web infrastructure, most of the FMIS developed in the last decade (149 of 176, or 84.7 %) are web-based solutions. The other 27 solutions (15.3 %) are usually legacy systems based on distributed architecture, and they run on a client-server platform (Figure 3.41).

Finally, the data set also includes information about the type of FMIS project initiated or completed in the 176 economies to install ICT solutions and provide advisory support for capacity building and change management. The systems used in 148 economies (84 %) were designed and implemented as a new turnkey solution (first time or replacing a previous system). About 23 systems (13.1 %) were developed as an improved or expanded version of existing FMIS solutions.

Figure 3.41 FMIS technology architecture

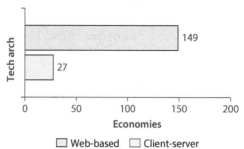

Source: World bank data
Note: FMIS = Financial Management Information System; COTS =
Commercial off the shelf software; LDSW = Locally Developed Software.

The remaining systems were implemented mainly in fragile states during emergency technical assistance projects by installing one of the COTS solutions for rapid deployment.

The websites did not yield detailed information about the duration and cost of implementation for most of the FMIS solutions. However, the World Bank's FMIS Database provides reliable information about the cost/duration and other important aspects (scope, functional modules, procurement approach, lessons learned, and so on) of about 109 projects funded by the World Bank in 60 countries (updated twice a year, last update in July 2013; see https://eteam.worldbank.org/FMIS for details).

Comparison of Findings with PEFA Indicators

The team used some of the Public Expenditure and Financial Accountability (PEFA) PFM Performance Measurement Framework indicators that are related to fiscal transparency in a comparative analysis with the findings of this study (see Appendix B for details). As of January 2013, the PEFA assessments were available for 121 economies, but only 65 countries published their PEFA results on the web; the disclosure of the PEFA results for 32 countries was not permitted by the governments, and these economies were excluded from this analysis. Although draft PEFA reports were available for the remaining 24 economies, their disclosure status was unknown.

The FMIS & OBD scores were compared with the PEFA indicators using the publicly available assessments for 65 economies. For this comparison, the PEFA indicator scores were converted to numbers from 1 to 4 (A=4; D=1; other scores—B+, B, C+, C, and D+—are equally distributed with increments of 0.5).

Two scatter diagrams were prepared to plot the correlation of 10 selected indicators, as well as the full set of PEFA indicators using average scores (NR/NA/NU scores, not rated, were excluded while calculating the averages):

- The average of PEFA scores for 10 selected indicators related to fiscal transparency (**Avg 10**) was compared with the FMIS & OBD scores.

Figure 3.42 Comparison of PEFA scores with FMIS & OBD scores (65 economies)

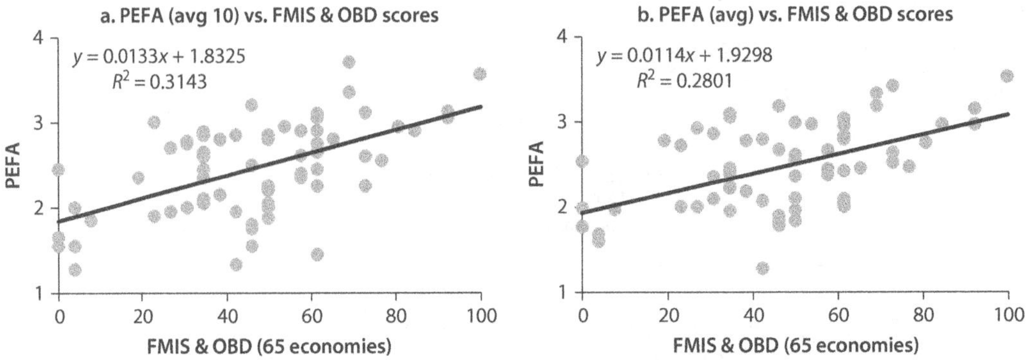

a. PEFA (avg 10) vs. FMIS & OBD scores

$y = 0.0133x + 1.8325$
$R^2 = 0.3143$

FMIS & OBD (65 economies)

b. PEFA (avg) vs. FMIS & OBD scores

$y = 0.0114x + 1.9298$
$R^2 = 0.2801$

FMIS & OBD (65 economies)

Source: World Bank data.
Note: Avg 10 means the average of 10 PEFA indicators selected for a comparison with the FMIS & OBD Scores. Avg means the average of all 31 PEFA indicators. NR/NA/NU scores are excluded in average calculations. PEFA = Public Expenditure and Financial Accountability; FMIS = Financial Management Information System; OBD = Open Budget Data.

- The average of all 31 PEFA scores (**Avg**) was compared with the FMIS & OBD scores.

Both diagrams demonstrate that there is a positive correlation between the FMIS & OBD scores and the PEFA scores in 65 economies, and the countries with higher PEFA scores tend to perform better in terms of publishing PF data and readiness to disclose open budget data from FMIS solutions (Figure 3.42). The trend observed for 10 selected PEFA indicators was very similar to the pattern for the whole set of PEFA indicators. This indicates that the FMIS & OBD scores capture consistent patterns for 65 economies compared to their performance in PEFA assessments.

As the next step, the FMIS & OBD scores were also compared with the full set of PEFA indicators available for 121 countries (Public+Final+Draft assessments) for a broader analysis. Individual country scores were not disclosed for final and draft reports. However, the average scores were used to prepare two additional scatter diagrams to plot the correlation of 10 selected indicators, as well as the full set of PEFA indicators, for all 121 economies (Figure 3.43).

These diagrams also indicate a positive correlation between the FMIS & OBD scores and the PEFA scores. The similar trends indicate that the results obtained from FMIS & OBD key indicators are largely consistent with the patterns observed through PEFA indicators.

Comparison with Open Budget Index

The 2012 Open Budget Survey (OBS) measures the state of budget transparency, participation, and oversight in 100 countries (see Appendix B for details). The OBS consists of 125 questions and is completed by independent researchers

Figure 3.43 Comparison of PEFA scores with FMIS & OBD scores (121 economies)

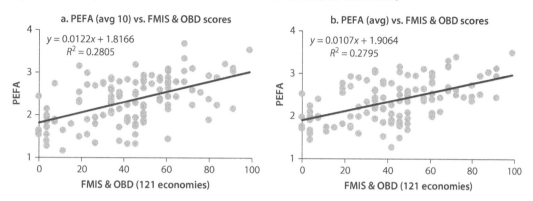

Source: World Bank data.
Note: Avg 10 means the average of 10 PEFA indicators selected for a comparison with the FMIS & OBD Scores. Avg means the average of all 31 PEFA indicators. NR/NA/NU scores are excluded in average calculations. PEFA = Public Expenditure and Financial Accountability; FMIS = Financial Management Information System; OBD = Open Budget Data.

in the countries assessed. The Open Budget Index (OBI) is calculated as a simple average of the responses for 95 questions that are related to budget transparency. The OBI assigns each country a score[1] that can range from 0 to 100. The OBS is useful in clarifying and comparing the contents of key budget documents in selected countries. However, it contains no questions about the source of information in published budget documents and the reliability/integrity of the underlying databases. FMIS & OBD indicators provide additional information on these less known aspects, as well as the visibility of open budget data, to complement the OBS.

The scatter diagram of the FMIS & OBD and OBI scores in 100 economies (Figure 3.44) reveals a positive correlation between these scores.

Table 3.3 summarizes the distribution of FMIS & OBD practice groups in 100 countries (with OBI scores) to clarify the patterns observed.

Most of the findings of the present study are consistent with the OBI scores, when the current status of government practices to publish open budget data (FMIS & OBD practice groups) is compared with the public availability and comprehensiveness of key budget documents (92 out of 100 countries, highlighted in shaded area). In only a few exceptional cases (outside the shaded area) do the economies perform better in terms of readiness to publish open budget data compared to their OBI score (for example, Bolivia and Ecuador within group A, and OBI scores 12 and 31, respectively). This may be due to the fact that, although they had a well-designed website and clear linkage between published open budget data and the underlying FMIS, the contents and types of budget documents they published were not adequate to get higher scores in OBI. Also, there are a few countries with no visibility on the web in terms of publishing budget data, but their OBI scores are above 40 (for example, Mali within group D, and OBI score 43). Most probably this was due to the fact that the OBI assessment is based on the review of submitted budget documents that are not disclosed on the web.

Figure 3.44 Comparison of OBI scores with FMIS & OBD scores (100 economies)

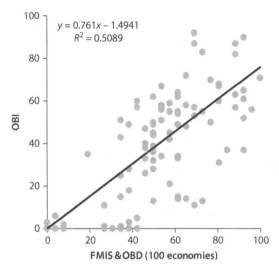

Source: World Bank data.
Note: FMIS = Financial Management Information System; OBI = Open Budget Index; OBD = Open Budget Data.

Table 3.3 Comparison of FMIS & OBD groups with OBI 2012 scores in 100 countries

OBI 2012	A	B	C	D	Total
0–20	1	4	13	8	26
21–40	1	12	1	1	15
41–60	7	23	5	1	36
61–80	10	7	—	—	17
81–100	4	2	—	—	6
Total	23	48	19	10	**100**

Source: World Bank data.
Note: OBI = Open Budget Index.

Ten countries have high OBI scores (above 60) and follow good practices (Group A) in publishing open budget data from FMIS: Brazil, Germany, Rep. of Korea, Mexico, New Zealand, Russian Federation, Spain, Sweden, the United Kingdom, the United States). In general, economies with higher OBI scores tend to perform much better in publishing open budget data from reliable FMIS databases, and those with lower OBI scores perform less well. *Thus, it appears that the indicators selected for this study consistently capture the main characteristics of PF websites that are relevant to the OBS questions.*

Comparison with Other Dimensions

As a final check on the validity of the findings, the team compared the FMIS & OBD scores with other relevant initiatives and dimensions—the Open Government Partnership, MTEF implementation, UN e-Government Development rankings, and Open Source Policies.

Table 3.4 Comparison of FMIS & OBD groups with OGP in 60 countries

OGP	A	B	C	D	Total
0 Developing commitments >	2	—	3	—	5
1 Commitments delivered >	14	33	7	1	55
Total	16	33	10	1	**60**

Source: World Bank data.
Note: OGP = Open Government Partnership; — = not available.

Table 3.5 Comparison of FMIS & OBD groups with MTEF implementation in 181 economies

MTEF (2010)	A	B	C	D	Total
0 No MTEF	4	10	20	15	49
1 MTFF	9	36	18	8	71
2 MTBF	7	22	10	3	42
3 MTPF	7	12	—	—	19
— Unknown	—	1	6	10	17
Total	27	81	54	36	**198**

Source: World Bank data.
Note: MTEF = Medium-Term Expenditure framework; MTFF = Medium-Term Fiscal Framework; MTBF = Medium-Term Budgeting Framework; MTPF = Medium-Term Performance Framework; — = not available.

Open Government Partnership

Open Government Partnership (OGP) was launched on September 20, 2011. Since then, 55 members joined the group by endorsing the declaration (as of June 2013); and 5 other countries are expected to officially endorse the declaration in 2013, and are in the process of developing commitments. Table 3.4 presents a comparison of the FMIS & OBD groups with the OGP participation status.

Most of the governments with endorsed declarations (47 out of 55) have high FMIS & OBD scores (Group A or B), and 11 governments have relatively low scores (Group C and D). It appears that most of the economies involved in OGP are getting ready for publishing open budget data from FMIS solutions to improve their PF web publishing practices.

Fourteen countries have endorsed the OGP declarations and already following good practices in publishing open budget data from FMIS solutions (Argentina, Brazil, Colombia, El Salvador, Guatemala, Republic of Korea, Mexico, Netherlands, Paraguay, Peru, Spain, Turkey, United Kingdom, and the United States). Two countries in Group A are in the process of developing commitments (Australia and Ireland).

Medium-Term Expenditure Framework Implementation

Drawing from the data set in a report published by the World Bank[2] on the adoption of the medium-term expenditure framework (MTEF) in 181 economies (1990–2010), the study team compared the findings of this study with the current status of MTEF implementation (see Table 3.5).

In the present study, MTEF is viewed as a sequence of three increasingly demanding stages: medium-term fiscal framework (MTFF), medium-term budgetary framework (MTBF), and medium-term performance framework (MTPF). Of the 19 countries implementing MTPF with an emphasis on the measurement and evaluation of budget performance, all consistently have high FMIS & OBD scores. A large number of governments (113) are included in the MTBF and MTFF, and many of them also have high FMIS & OBD scores. Even of the 49 economies that have no MTEF implementation, 4 have relatively high FMIS & OBD scores (Bolivia, Ecuador, El Salvador, and Guatemala in Group A). This indicates that there is a parallel between the implementation of MTEF at various stages and the publication of open budget data from reliable FMIS databases. However, some of the governments with no MTEF focus can still publish substantial budget data to present the performance of their budget implementation (plans vs. actuals; results) and provide useful feedback for the evaluation of their budget.

UN e-Government Development Rankings 2012

The overall conclusion of the UN's e-Government 2012 survey is that *"governments must increasingly begin to rethink in terms of e-government—and e-governance—placing greater emphasis on institutional linkages between and among the tiered government structures in a bid to create synergy for inclusive sustainable development, by widening the scope of e-Gov for a transformative role towards cohesive, coordinated, and integrated processes and institutions."* In the PFM domain, such a transformation is possible through reliable FMIS solutions that provide timely information to a large number of budget users. Therefore, the e-Gov development ranking is another relevant measure of readiness to publish open budget data from FMIS, in terms of online services, ICT infrastructure, and human capital.

Table 3.6 presents the distribution of FMIS & OBD groups in 190 economies included in the UN 2012 e-Government Development rankings. In terms of both e-Gov'12 ranking and index values, the FMIS & OBD scores follow consistent patterns in most of these economies

About 90 % of the 40 countries with the top e-Government rankings are in Group A or B regarding their current practices in publishing open budget data. The FMIS & OBD groups shift toward C and D as the e-Gov rankings decline. A small number of economies are exceptions to this trend (15 out of 190, or

Table 3.6 Comparison of FMIS & OBD groups with e-Gov'12 rankings and indices

eGov rank	A	B	C	D	Total	eGov index	A	B	C	D	Total
1–40	13	23	2	2	40	0.00–0.20	—	3	3	4	10
41–80	7	18	12	3	40	0.21–0.40	2	16	23	17	58
81–120	5	18	10	7	40	0.41–0.60	7	29	17	7	60
121–160	2	13	15	10	40	0.61–0.80	9	22	8	4	43
161–190	—	6	13	11	30	0.81–1.00	9	8	1	1	19
Total	27	78	52	33	**190**	**Total**	27	78	52	33	**190**

Source: World Bank data.
Note: — = not available.

8 %); however, most of the economies display a consistent pattern in FMIS & OBD groupings and e-Gov rankings. As regards the e-Gov indices, more than 90 % of the countries in each index interval display consistent patterns, and only 11 out of 190 economies are outside the shaded area representing the trend.

EGDI. The e-Government Development Index (EGDI) is a composite indicator measuring governments' willingness and capacity to use ICT in the delivery of public services. The EGDI is a weighted average of three normalized scores on the most important dimensions:

- Scope and quality of online services
- Development status of telecommunication infrastructure
- Inherent human capital.

The four stages of online service development are defined as (a) emerging, (b) enhanced, (c) transactional, and (d) connected (with increasing level of sophistication). Only about 23 % of the economies (43 out of 190) have EGDI scores above 0.60 for connected or transactional online services, with relatively high FMIS & OBD groups. A vast majority of the countries provide emerging or enhanced services through their websites, and this is consistent with the findings of this study (Table 3.7).

Telco infrastructure index. The telecommunication (Telco) infrastructure index is an arithmetic average of five indicators per 100 inhabitants: (a) estimated Internet users, (b) number of main fixed telephone lines, (c) number of mobile subscribers, (d) number of fixed internet subscriptions, and (e) number of fixed broadband facilities. The International Telecommunication Union is the primary source of data in each case. Table 3.8 presents the comparison of FMIS & OBD groups with the Telco infrastructure index.

Table 3.7 Comparison of FMIS & OBD groups with e-Gov'12 index (Online Services)

eGov'12 (OS)	A	B	C	D	Total
0.00–0.20	—	4	10	19	33
0.21–0.40	1	20	29	10	60
0.41–0.60	9	32	10	3	54
0.61–0.80	9	12	3	1	25
0.81–1.00	8	10	—	—	18
Total	27	78	52	33	**190**

Source: World Bank data.
Note: — = not available.

Table 3.8 Comparison of FMIS & OBD groups with e-Gov'12 index (Telco Infrastructure)

eGov'12 (TI)	A	B	C	D	Total
0.00–0.20	4	24	29	22	79
0.21–0.40	8	23	9	3	43
0.41–0.60	3	14	9	5	31
0.61–0.80	9	13	4	1	27
0.81–1.00	3	4	1	2	10
Total	27	78	52	33	**190**

Source: World Bank data.

Only about 37 out of 190 (19 %) of the economies have EGDI scores above 0.60 for the telecommunication infrastructure index. However, most of the countries have inadequate Internet connectivity and broadband access, and this is another important aspect to consider in analyzing the relatively lower FMIS & OBD scores in these economies.

Human capital index. The human capital index is a weighted average of two indicators: (a) adult literacy rate, and (b) the combined primary, secondary, and tertiary gross enrollment ratio; a two-thirds weight is assigned to adult literacy rate, and one-third to the gross enrollment ratio. The distribution of FMIS & OBD groups with respect to the EGDI index for human capital is presented in Table 3.9. It appears that most of the economies (142 out of 190, or 75 %) score above 0.60, and have relatively high FMIS & OBD groups. Most of the countries are scattered along the trend line indicated by the shaded area in the table.

In summary, the findings of this study are largely consistent with the EGDI indices. The human capital index is high in most of the countries, but the online service and Telco infrastructure indices are high only in about 20 % of the economies where the FMIS & OBD groups are also high, indicating a much better level of readiness to publish open budget data, in line with the EGDI indices.

Open Source Policies

The seventh update to the CSIS Open Source Policy Survey[3] was published in 2010. The survey tracks government policies on the use of open source software (OSS). The survey is divided into four categories: (a) research and development, (b) mandates (where the use of OSS is required), (c) preferences (where the use of OSS is given preference, but not mandated), and (d) advisory (where the use of OSS is permitted). The survey also looks at whether an initiative was made at the national, regional, or local level, and whether it was accepted, under consideration, or rejected.

The study has found a total of 362 open source policy initiatives (Table 3.10), of which 227 are at the national level (66 economies), 117 are at the state or local level (22 economies), and 18 at the international level (EU, OECD, UN). About 69 % of these open source policies have been approved (Table 3.11). The survey results show a greater tendency for the approval of open source research and development initiatives relative to mandatory, preference, or advisory policies.

Table 3.9 Comparison of FMIS & OBD groups with e-Gov'12 index (Human Capital)

eGov'12 (HC)	A	B	C	D	Total
0.00–0.20	—	1	—	3	4
0.21–0.40	—	3	7	3	13
0.41–0.60	1	13	11	6	31
0.61–0.80	7	20	15	10	52
0.81–1.00	19	41	19	11	90
Total	27	78	52	33	**190**

Source: World Bank data.
Note: — = not available.

Table 3.10 Scope and regional distribution of open source policies

Scope of policy	R&D	Advisory	Preference	Mandatory	Total
National	69	66	60	32	227
State/Local	25	19	52	21	117
International	5	12	1	—	18
Total	99	97	113	53	**362**

Region	Approved	Proposed	Failed	Total
Europe	126	35	10	171
Asia	59	20	2	81
Latin America	31	15	11	57
North America	16	11	10	37
Africa	8	1	0	9
Middle East	5	2	0	7
Total	245	84	33	**362**

Source: World Bank data.
Note: — = not available.

Table 3.11 Regional distribution of approved open source initiatives

Region	R&D	Advisory	Preference	Mandatory	Total
Europe	45	37	36	8	126
Asia	19	16	22	2	59
Latin America	8	6	12	5	31
North America	5	8	2	1	16
Africa	3	1	4	0	8
Middle East	1	2	2	0	5
Total	81	70	78	16	**245**

Source: World Bank data.

Table 3.12 Distribution of FMIS & OBD groups in 66 economies with open source policies

OSS Policies/FMIS & OBD Groups >	A	B	C	D
National-level: 66 economies >	22	**38**	4	2
State/local-level: 22 economies >	10	**12**	—	—

Source: World Bank data.
Note: OSS = Open Source Software; FMIS = Financial Management Information System; OBD = Open Budget Data;
— = not available.

Table 3.12 shows the distribution of FMIS & OBD groups for national- and state/local-level open source policies. This indicates that there is a positive correlation between the FMIS & OBD groups and the use of open source policies in the public sector, which in turn promotes the publication of open budget data. At the national level, 60 out of 66 governments (91 %) follow good practices in this regard. For the state/local level, all of the 22 economies with open source policies have high FMIS & OBD scores.

Financial Management Information Systems and Open Budget Data
http://dx.doi.org/10.1596/978-1-4648-0083-2

> With these and earlier comparative analyses, it can be concluded that the indicators defined for this study produce consistent results when compared to other relevant indicators of data transparency.

Notes

1. OBI: 0–20: Scant or no info | 21–40: Minimal | 41–60: Some | 61–80: Significant | 81–100: Extensive.
2. "Beyond the annual budget: Global experience with medium-term expenditure frameworks," World Bank, September 2012. doi:10.1596/978-0-8213-9625-4 License: Creative Commons Attribution CC BY 3.0.
3. CSIS Open Source Policy Survey, 2010.

CHAPTER 4

Good Practices

The findings of this study indicate that, although 198 governments around the world use 176 financial management information systems (FMIS) platforms, good practices in presenting open budget data from reliable FMIS solutions are highly visible in only about 24 countries (12%).

For this study, a *good practice* can be defined simply as publishing extensive, reliable, and timely public finance (PF) information, drawn from an FMIS, on easy-to-navigate government websites with dynamic query and reporting options. The purpose of identifying good practices is to allow users to learn from others performing well in different areas of publishing PF data, and to share relevant knowledge.

This chapter provides an overview of selected cases from all FMIS & open budget data (OBD) practice groups to share information about good practices in effectively addressing the challenges linked with open budget data and transparency. The last section of this chapter describes the FMIS World Map, a geomapping application developed on Google Maps to improve the visibility of the findings of this study.

In selecting the good practice cases, the following criteria were applied:

- Timely publication (I-1): A tradition of regularly publishing consistent PF information through dedicated websites
- Visibility of FMIS (I-2): Comprehensive information about the underlying FMIS solution or data warehouse (DW) used for publishing PF information
- Dynamic query options (I-3): Access to information for all revenues, allocations, and expenditures through user-defined (dynamic) queries on FMIS databases or DW
- Open budget data (I-4): Presenting a rich set of open budget data published from FMIS.

Some cases demonstrate that even in difficult settings innovative solutions to improve budget transparency can be developed rapidly with a modest investment, if there is political will and commitment from the government.

- Reliability of PF data (I-5 and I-6): Visibility of system name/time stamp on published reports
- Presentation quality (I-7 I-8): Presence of interactive and user-friendly graphical interfaces to display budget data and provide adequate search/download options
- Effective use of open data (I-9): Meaningful open data on fiscal policy, budget performance, and achievements available to the public (Citizens Budget).

Selected cases from all Regions are presented for each of the good practice categories listed, along with images from PF publication websites and relevant uniform resource locators (URLs) (100 cases from 53 government websites). Important characteristics of highly visible integrated FMIS solutions, including the Digital Budget and Accounting System (or DBAS)[1] and other sustained/emerging platforms (for example, Brazil, the Russian Federation), are also presented. Table 4.1 shows the distribution of good practice cases according to income levels, geographical locations, and FMIS & OBD groups.

Table 4.1 Good practices in publishing PF information/open budget data

Income Level	#	Government websites selected to highlight some of the good practices
High income	20	Australia; Austria; Taiwan, China; Denmark; Estonia; Finland; France; Germany; Ireland; Japan; Republic of Korea; Netherlands; New Zealand; Norway; Singapore; Slovenia; Spain; Sweden; United Kingdom; United States
Upper-middle income	17	Argentina; Brazil; Chile; China; Colombia; Dominican Rep.; Ecuador; Jordan; Malaysia; Mauritius; Mexico; Peru; Russian Fed.; Thailand; Turkey; Uruguay; Venezuela; RB
Lower-middle income	12	Bolivia; Guatemala; El Salvador; India; Indonesia; Morocco; Nicaragua; Pakistan; Paraguay; Philippines; Vietnam; Zambia
Low income	4	Madagascar; The Gambia; Timor-Leste; West Bank and Gaza
Region	#	Government websites selected to highlight some of the good practices
Africa	4	Madagascar; Mauritius; The Gambia; Zambia
East Asia and Pacific	13	Australia, China; Taiwan, China; Indonesia; Japan; Malaysia; New Zealand; Republic of Korea; Philippines; Singapore; Thailand; Timor-Leste; Vietnam
Europe and Central Asia	15	Austria; Denmark; Estonia; Finland; France; Germany; Ireland; Netherlands; Norway; Russian Federation; Slovenia; Spain; Sweden; Turkey; United Kingdom
North and South America	16	Argentina; Bolivia; Brazil; Chile; Colombia; Dominican Republic; Ecuador; El Salvador; Guatemala; Mexico; Nicaragua; Paraguay; Peru; Uruguay; United States; Venezuela; RB
Middle East and North Africa	3	Jordan; Morocco; West Bank and Gaza
South Asia	2	India; Pakistan

table continues next page

Table 4.1 Good practices in publishing PF information/open budget data *(continued)*

FMIS & OBD Group	#	Government websites selected to highlight some of the good practices
A	24	Argentina; Australia; Brazil; Colombia; Ecuador; El Salvador; Germany; Guatemala; India; Ireland; Republic of Korea; Mexico; Netherlands; New Zealand; Nicaragua; Paraguay; Peru; Russian Federation; Singapore; Slovenia; Spain; Turkey; United Kingdom; United States
B	26	Austria; Bolivia; Chile; China; Denmark; Dominican Republic; Estonia; Finland; France; Indonesia; Japan; Jordan; Madagascar; Malaysia; Mauritius; Morocco; Norway; Pakistan; Philippines; Sweden; Thailand; Timor-Leste; Uruguay; Vietnam; Venezuela, RB; Zambia
C	3	Taiwan, China; The Gambia; West Bank and Gaza

Source: World Bank data.
Note: FMIS = Financial Management Information System; OBD = Open Budget Data.

The following sections describe the examples. Relevant web links are available in the FMIS & OBD data set posted on the FMIS CoP website: https://eteam. worldbank.org/FMIS.

Timely Publication of PF Data through Dedicated Websites

A large number of PF websites provide historical information about the approved annual budget plans (153 out of 198, or 77 %) and budget execution results (147 out of 198, or 74 %). However, only about 60 % of these economies follow good practices and publish regularly: their performance in publishing the medium-term expenditure framework (MTEF) and investment plans, as well as the external audit of the budget, is well below the expected levels (see Table 4.2).

Although most of these PF websites have been created within the last decade, some of them provide a great amount of historical PF information. Brazil stands out as the best performer in this category, making available annual budget plans and budget execution results since 1980. Several other countries in Latin America and Caribbean Region (LCR) also present historical PF data since the 1980s (Argentina, Chile), but most of the governments publish data covering the last decade.

Government websites described in this section illustrate some of the good practices observed during this study, along with ongoing improvements linked with open budget data initiatives.

Table 4.2 Historical trends and regularity in publishing PF information

Since	Budget plans		MTEF		Investment plans		Budget execution		External audit	
	# Econ	Regular	# Econ	Regular	# Econ	Regular	# Econ	Regular	# Econ	Regular
1980	3	3	0	0	0	0	2	1	0	0
1990	29	29	12	12	6	6	27	27	13	13
2000	104	80	58	44	30	22	103	81	54	45
2010	17	8	33	8	8	4	15	8	8	2
Totals	153	120	103	64	44	32	147	117	75	60
%	77%	61%	52%	32%	22%	16%	74%	59%	38%	30%

Source: World Bank data.
Note: MTEF = Medium-Term Expenditure Framework.

Financial Management Information Systems and Open Budget Data
http://dx.doi.org/10.1596/978-1-4648-0083-2

Africa
Mauritius

The Ministry of Finance and Economic Development/Ministère des Finances et du Développement Économique website (http://www.mof.mu) presents key information about the organization, current and past national budget, legislation, and public debt. The budget section includes program-based budget estimates and actuals, as well as the public sector investment program online system, providing comprehensive information. Documents can be downloaded in PDF, DOC, or XLS formats.

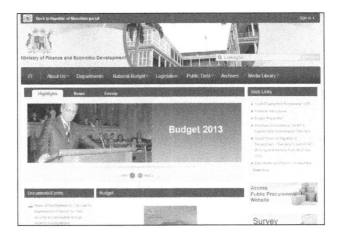

East Asia and Pacific
Australia

The Central Budget website is the entry point for Australian Government budget material (http://www.budget.gov.au). A rich set of budget information is available: budget speech, strategy, details of revenues and expenditures, appropriations, portfolio statements, execution performance, midyear economic and fiscal outlook, and final budget outcome. The past budgets section presents similar details for budget performance starting from 1996. Most of the reports are available in PDF format.

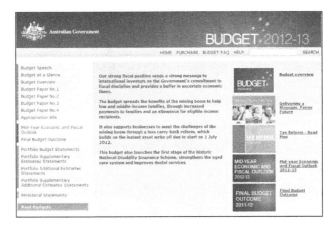

Japan

The Ministry of Finance (http://www.mof.go.jp) website presents key PF information in open data format. Policy documents, net total budget and balance sheet, budget execution performance, and treasury operations are published in PDF, XML, or XLS formats. Some of the government financial statistics are also available from the Statistics (e-Stat) website in open data formats (PDF, CSV, XLS, DB). The Ministry home page also includes web links to relevant government institutions, daily news, and feedback options for citizens and businesses.

Republic of Korea

The Ministry of Strategy and Finance website (http://www.mosf.go.kr) provides extensive information about economic policy, performance indicators, publications, budget execution performance, and e-applications. Other important features are web links to the Digital Budget and Accounting System (DBAS/dBrain); Treasury bonds; online bidding; statistical information; educational material for children, youth, and researchers; access to information policy; and submission of complaints.

New Zealand

The New Zealand Treasury/Kaitohutohu Kaupapa Rawa website (http://www.treasury.govt.nz) provides access to extensive information about government finances, budget performance, economy, state sector, and financial statistics. The home page is easy to navigate and includes links to important PF websites. A Treasury Twitter feed, quick links, and topics of current interest sections provide useful feedback for citizens and businesses. A mobile budget site and fiscal time series (1972–2012) present a rich set of open budget data and meaningful information on public finances.

Singapore

The Ministry of Finance (http://www.mof.gov.sg) home page is easy to navigate and provides extensive information about the budget process. Budget archives present the details of policies, public spending, and results since 1996. Individuals, civil society, and businesses can post their views and suggestions through a public consultation section. Mobile applications can be downloaded from the website to learn more about the details of budget plans and execution performance. A budget quiz and download pages provide additional information in an easy-to-understand format.

Europe and Central Asia
France
The Ministry of Economy and Finance/Ministère de l'Économie et des Finances website (http://www.economie.gouv.fr) provides direct access to regularly updated PF information. Public consultation and communication options include links to social media and WebTV. The budget and public finance website includes Performance Forum, where detailed information on budget performance and results is posted regularly in meaningful formats. The General Directorate of Treasury/Direction Générale du Trésor (http://www.tresor.economie.gouv.fr) website presents comprehensive data on the treasury and debt management.

Germany
The Ministry of Finance/Bundesministerium der Finanzen website (http://www.bundesfinanzministerium.de) provides, and frequently updates, extensive information on the federal budget. A services website provides access to key units, data, and reports and strategy documents. The home page has a number of options for communication with citizens and businesses (video, graphics, audio, and pictures) to convey key messages and share progress in ongoing reform activities. Budget execution performance is reported monthly.

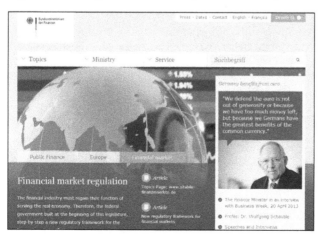

Financial Management Information Systems and Open Budget Data
http://dx.doi.org/10.1596/978-1-4648-0083-2

Russian Federation

The Ministry of Finance home page (http://www.minfin.ru) provides access to comprehensive information about the budget, pension, and local government reform activities, reserve and national wealth funds, budget execution performance, public debt, and audit results. Links to federal agency websites allow users to view and download a rich set of open budget data. The multiyear budget framework is presented, along with updates on the regulations related to specific activities and the description of all MoF information systems. The new budget portal (pilot) is impressive (www.budget.gov.ru).

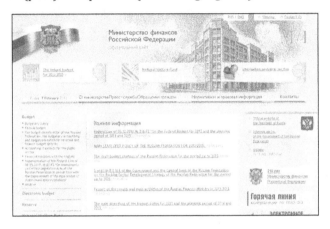

Sweden

The Ministry of Finance (MoF) website presents (http://www.sweden.gov.se) the responsibilities, key program activities, news, and publications of the Ministry. Detailed information about the national economy and budget is posted under the "policy areas" section of the website. The MoF web page also includes the financial stability framework, latest legislation, links to relevant agencies, and several interaction options for citizens and businesses. The latest PF forecasts, as well as a follow-up of budget policy objectives and estimate for expenditure ceiling, are also presented through relevant web pages and documents.

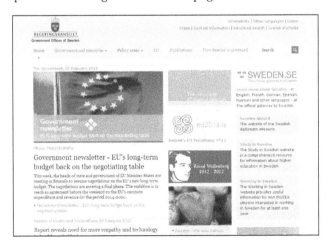

North and South America
Argentina
The Ministry of Economy and Public Finance/Ministerio de Economía y Finanzas Públicas (MECON) (http://www.mecon.gov.ar) is the main source of PF information in Argentina. The website is easy to navigate and provides comprehensive information about the organization, relevant legislation, programs, budget performance, and such other important aspects as file queries, documentation and information center, innovation, and tenders. The InfoLEG (Información Legislativa y Documental) section provides online access to all relevant legal documents.

Brazil
The Brazilian Ministry of Finance/Ministério da Fazenda (http://www.fazenda.gov.br) has one of the most comprehensive federal government websites, providing a rich set of information on all aspects, as well as links to a large number of internal and external PF sites. The National Treasury/Tesouro Nacional has a contemporary website (https://www.tesouro.fazenda.gov.br) publishing detailed budget execution reports from the new FMIS, SIAFI. To improve the efficiency of public spending, a data warehouse extracts data from SIAPE, SIAFI, and SIGPLAN to generate information for decision support and performance monitoring.

Another important source of information is the Federal Budget portal, maintained by the Ministry of Planning and Budget Management/Ministério do Planejamento, Orçamento e Gestão (http://www.planejamento.gov.br). The portal provides access to federal budget and investment plans, Program for Accelerated Growth/Programa de Aceleração do Crescimento, and multiyear plans.

Chile

The Ministry of Finance/Ministerio de Hacienda (http://www.hacienda.cl) website presents comprehensive information about PF benefits, procedures, and programs, as well as fiscal transparency activities. There is a dedicated web page for citizen participation in policy formulation and execution. The Documents section includes web links to all historical and current data about the budget plans and execution performance obtained from Sistema de Información para la Gestión Financiera del Estado (SIGFE) databases.

Colombia

The Ministry of Finance and Public Credit/Ministerio de Hacienda y Crédito Público (http://www.minhacienda.gov.co) maintains an informative and easy-to-navigate website to present substantial information about public finances. Links to SIIF Nation and a Transparency Portal provide access to detailed information about central and local budget activities, including the performance of budget execution, revenue collection and spending details, progress in investments, and the details of all major contracts signed.

Ecuador

The Ministry of Finance/Ministerio de Finanzas (http://www.finanzas.gob.ec) home page presents comprehensive information about the status of PF and historical trends in an easy-to-understand format. Links to SIGEF (Sistema Integrado de Gestion Financiera) and the Government Results/Gobierno por Resultados portal provide access to detailed information on sectoral and departmental spending and revenues. The Ministry website includes a large amount of multimedia content (YouTube, presentations, SIGEF e-Learning platform) to inform citizens and civil society with clear and easy-to-understand messages.

Financial Management Information Systems and Open Budget Data
http://dx.doi.org/10.1596/978-1-4648-0083-2

Mexico

The Ministry of Finance and Public Credit/Secretaría de Hacienda y Crédito Publico website (http://www.shcp.gob.mx) presents extensive information about PF, budget revenues and expenditures, treasury operations, regulations, and budget transparency. A number of feedback mechanisms are provided for citizens and businesses through a transparency portal and access to information (InfoMex) sites. Information on federal government contracts, reports, wages, regulations, subsidies, services, concessions, and permits issued are also provided. Dynamic query options are available to present reports from PF databases.

Middle East and North Africa
Morocco

The Ministry of Economy and Finance/Le Ministère de l'Economie et des Finances portal (http://www.finances.gov.ma) provides access to key PF information and timely updates on state budget execution, regulations, and public debt. A gender-responsive budget section and links to PF agencies also present open budget data. The General Treasury/Trésorerie Generale website presents the details of public spending and taxes, along with e-services and forms. Historical data are available from the databases and documents section.

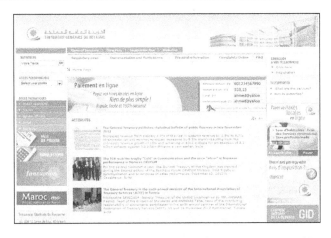

South Asia
India

The Ministry of Finance regularly presents comprehensive data (http://www.finmin.nic.in) on the Indian state budget, PF statistics, public debt, tenders, and monthly economic reports. The government accounting and reporting functions are supported through the e-Lekha solution, developed by the National Informatics Center for the office of the Controller General of Accounts. Most of the budget execution reports are produced and posted from e-Lekha. Reports posted on the MoF website can be viewed or downloaded in PDF.

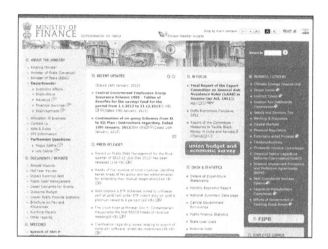

Visibility of FMIS Solutions on the Web

This section highlights some of the websites that present the key features of the FMIS that is used in publishing PF information.

Africa
Madagascar

The Ministry of Finance and Budget (MoFB) maintains a dedicated website for introducing the Integrated Public Financial Management System/Système Intégré de Gestion des Finances Publiques (SIGFIP). The website describes the functional modules and users of the system, provides web links to other Public Finance Management (PFM) systems, and explains the history of the system's development and the units responsible for managing the system. The MoFB maintains the SIGFIP platform to facilitate data exchange among a number of fragmented information systems.

Financial Management Information Systems and Open Budget Data
http://dx.doi.org/10.1596/978-1-4648-0083-2

East Asia and Pacific
Australia
The Central Budget Management System website presents the details of Australia's new integrated FMIS development process. The background of the project and current status are explained in detail, as are the expected benefits and the changes introduced through the new system. The website provides timely feedback to all stakeholders about the stages of system implementation, and supports the change management activities. Presentations and various feedback mechanisms are also available to improve communication and coordination.

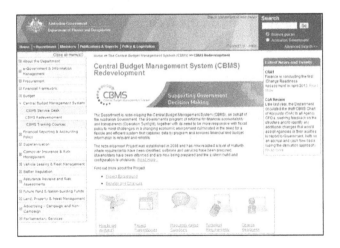

Indonesia
The Ministry of Finance's dedicated website (http://www.depkeu.go.id) presents the main features and development phases of the SPAN (State Treasury and Budgetary System/Sistem Perbendaharaan dan Anggaran Negara) solution,

which is expected to be operational in 2014. The SPAN website, built on a content management platform, provides useful updates on massive change management activities, as well as blog posts, news, and announcements of upcoming events. When SPAN is operational, it will be the source of PF information.

Republic of Korea

The Digital Budget and Accounting System (DBAS) website (https://www.digitalbrain.gov.kr) provides access to extensive PF information and open budget data. DBAS or dBrain system modules and the history of system development are presented in detail. Information about the PF policy, medium-term fiscal plan, budget system, government securities, cash management, procurement/tenders, and financial statistics is presented in a user-friendly format and updated regularly. Citizens/businesses can submit questions and download reports in various formats.

Financial Management Information Systems and Open Budget Data
http://dx.doi.org/10.1596/978-1-4648-0083-2

Malaysia

The Government Financial and Management Accounting System (GFMAS) is the accounting system used by the Accountant General Department since 2006. The GFMAS website presents the capabilities of this integrated system (financial planning, budget control, and government accounting). Salary management, government loans, investments, and the preparation of public accounts are also covered. Online statistics system and data-mart sections provide useful information about the status of budget execution, as well as historical PF data.

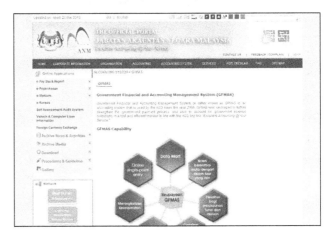

Europe and Central Asia
France

CHORUS is an integrated FMIS solution (based on SAP) that supports financial, budgetary, and accounting management at central and decentralized levels. The CHORUS website presents detailed information about the history of development and system functionality. The system provides timely and reliable PF information to all departments and programs. Another important source of PF information is the Open Government Data portal (http://www.data.gouv.fr).

Russian Federation

The Ministry of Finance uses a dedicated website to regularly present developments related to the design and implementation of a new integrated FMIS solution (e-Budget). The legal and regulatory framework, status of implementation, work plans, system functionality, and working group activities are published, together with updates on the development of a single budget portal, state and municipal payment system, and other components. The new e-Budget system is expected to be operational in 2016. Currently, most of the open budget data is published from Federal Treasury Automation System databases.

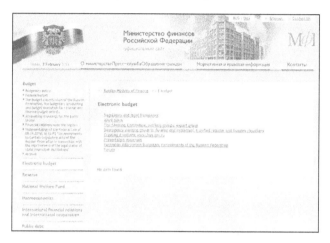

The United Kingdom

The Online System for Central Accounting and Reporting (OSCAR) website provides access to extensive open budget data extracted from a public spending database. This data set makes public spending data more directly accessible and can be used with standard spreadsheet software. OSCAR is designed as a user-friendly system to provide the Treasury with key management information and data for public reporting. The system appears to be fully operational, and data covering the first six months of 2012–13 (April-September) have recently been published.

North and South America

Argentina

The Sistema Integrado de Información Financiera (SIDIF) web page provides detailed information about Argentina's FMIS. The system's conceptual model, functionality, scope, history of development and upgrades, training manuals, and interfaces with other systems are presented clearly. The website also has options for requesting information, following SIDIF events, and participating in relevant courses. The SIDIF website is updated regularly with information about developments and good practices. SIDIF is the source of the PF information that is published on the MECON website.

Bolivia

The Ministry of Economy and Public Finance/Ministerio de Economía y Finanzas Públicas (http://www.economiayfinanzas.gob.bo) home page is easy to navigate and provides access to personnel data, contracts, publications, legal framework, and links to other units. Detailed budget information since 2000 is published from SIGMA (Sistema Integrado de Gestión y Modernización Administrativa). In addition to improving transparency in resource management, SIGMA provides timely and reliable information, interacts with the planning system and public investments, and provides feedback to the results tracking system.

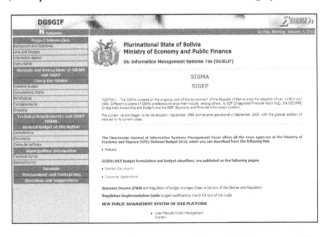

Brazil

SIAFI is the Integrated System of Financial Administration of Brazil's Federal Government (Sistema Integrado de Administração Financeira). Operational since 1987 and thus one of the oldest FMIS solutions around, SIAFI was developed to support budget execution, accounting, and reporting. The new SIAFI is a web-based application (operational since January 2012) to which all SIAFI modules will gradually migrate. It is compliant with the Federal Government's interoperability standards (e-ping). The new SIAFI includes the Accounts Payable and Receivable module. SIAFI websites present the system functionality, reports, and dynamic query options.

The SIOP (Sistema de Presupuesto y Planeamiento) portal provides access to the Federal Government's new budget preparation system (which is based on open source software and freely available to Brazilian states. Monthly, quarterly, or annual budget reports can be downloaded for current and previous years.

Chile

Sistema de Información para la Gestión Financiera del Estado (SIGFE) has been operational in Chile since 2007. The new version is a hybrid solution combining budget preparation (based on COTS) and execution locally developed software (LDSW) modules to support key functions, including the daily monitoring of all revenues and expenditures, cash management, the monitoring of multiyear commitments and budget programs, and the management of documents and workflow (supporting electronic documents).

Nicaragua

Sistema Integrado de Gestión Financiera (SIGFA), operational since 2002, was upgraded to a web-enabled system in 2009 to support budget preparation, execution, accounting, and reporting. The Ministry of Finance is in the process of selecting the new web-based FMIS solution to support PFM reforms and new requirements. The SIGFA website presents useful information about the PFM reforms (since 1996), and about the e-SIGFA platform, which integrates SIGFA with other PFM systems.

Venezuela

The Integrated System for Administration and Control of Public Finances/ Sistema Integrado de Gestión y Control de las Finanzas Públicas (SIGECOF) supports budget preparation, execution, and reporting functions. The system is linked with the Debt Management System and Public Investment Management to provide useful information about budget execution performance through the Ministry of Planning and Finance website. The history of system development, legal basis, and digital library are accessible from the SIGECOF website.

Middle East and North Africa
Jordan

The Ministry of Finance (http://www.mof.gov.jo) initiated the development of the Government Financial Management Information System (GFMIS, http://www.gfmis.gov.jo) in 2005, to support budget preparation, execution, accounting, and reporting. GFMIS development was completed in 2012, and the system is expected to be operational in 2013. The GFMIS website presents the history of system development and related publications and change management activities. GFMIS is expected to be the source of PF information for publishing online.

South Asia
India
The Controller General of Accounts (CGA) maintains e-Lekha as a management accounting system for all levels. The system is mainly used for payments and public account transactions, centralized maintenance of the CoA, and cash management. The Central Plan Scheme Monitoring System (CPSMS) was introduced in 2011 to monitor all funds releases and payments countrywide (gradually expanding to all states by 2018), and included interfaces with Core Banking Solutions for payments. The CGA is now moving toward an integrated FMIS solution (GFMIS) to link budget preparation, execution, accounting, and reporting.

Pakistan
The Financial Accounting and Budgeting System, developed by Pakistan Audit Department under the PIFRA (Project to Improve Financial Reporting and Auditing), supports budget execution, accounting, and reporting. The PIFRA website provides useful information about the objectives, expected results, functional modules, cost, and components of the project. The first phase of the project was completed in 2004 and the second phase, including the rollout of a payroll module, in 2011.

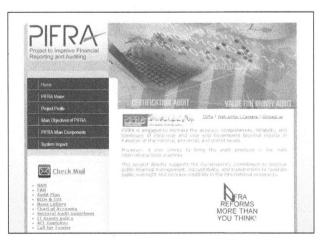

Access to PF Information through Dynamic Query Options

This section describes good practice cases linked with access to PF data through dynamic query options to generate user-defined or predefined reports from FMIS databases.

East Asia and Pacific
China

The Ministry of Finance maintains a comprehensive website for publishing PF data (http://www.mof.gov.cn/) on central and local government activities. Dynamic query options are available for generating reports on central budget revenues and expenditures, monitoring the performance of local budgets, and retrieving historical data on national financial accounts. There is also a section on public participation, as well as online services (to download forms and reports) and updates on ongoing PFM reforms.

Timor-Leste

The Timor-Leste Budget Transparency Portal provides extensive information on the execution of the national budget. The portal is updated daily from underlying FMIS databases, and is accessible to the public, civil society, and development partners. The portal provides a large number of dynamic query options to monitor the budget (plans, actuals, commitments, obligations), and reports may be downloaded in various formats (PDF, DOC, XLS, XML, and HTML).

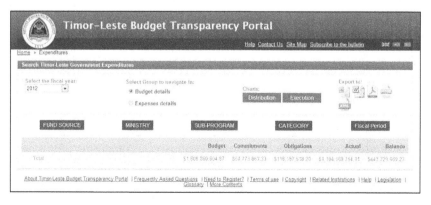

Europe and Central Asia
Denmark

The Ministry of Finance/Finansministeriet website (http://uk.fm.dk) includes a section on publications and a dynamic query window through which users can drill down on public spending details for each institution. The FMIS solution is the source of information for the PF database, and it is possible to select a specific budget program level and entity to produce a listing of relevant spending (plans vs. actuals). The query filter is displayed, together with the level of report detail, at the top of the window. Displayed open budget data can be downloaded in CSV format.

Estonia

The Ministry of Finance/Rahandusministeerium website (http://www.fin.ee/ riigieelarve) presents the overall status of budget execution through consolidated results for the government sector, which consists of about 3,100 institutions, including nearly 2,700 local governments. The details of budget activities are available from the Statistics Estonia website and databases. Revenue, expenditure and general government debt can be monitored in detail from the Statistics database, with a rich set of query and filtering options.

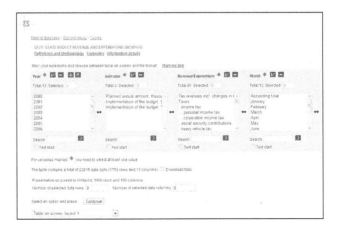

The Netherlands

The Ministry of Finance/De Rijksoverheid home page presents, and regularly updates, a comprehensive set of Documents and Publications on budget performance. User-defined search/query options can be specified to extract relevant publications according to ministry or report types, and there are options to refine the search results. Budget documents, annual plans, guidelines, and other reports can be selected and downloaded as PDF or XLS files from the archives. Reports on the state budget, taxes, and other public finance information can also be obtained from the National Budget web page.

Turkey

The Ministry of Finance eBudget/eBütçe website provides access to extensive open budget data from PF databases. User-defined or standard reports can be generated online and downloaded in various forms (XLS, PDF). Dynamic query options are provided to specify the reporting period, type of report, and budget institutions, and to select desired budget classification segments, as well as the rows/columns to be displayed. The portal is used for public access as well as secure internal access by government officials.

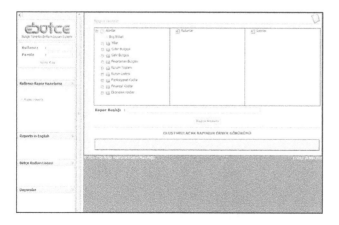

North and South America

Argentina

The Ministry of Economy and Public Finance (MECON) has a dedicated web-page to present key public finance information, with dynamic query options. Selected open budget data can be displayed on the screen or downloaded (PDF, RTF) for further analysis. The reports indicate the source of information (Business Intelligence database) and include the date/time stamp for the creation of files. The MECON Information web page provides direct access to all important PF information, with clear explanations about the scope and period covered.

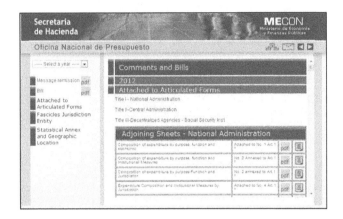

Bolivia

The Ministry of Economy and Public Finance provides dynamic query options for access to a number of budget documents—for example, executive branch financial statements (since 1991) and balance sheets and other reports of financial institutions (since 2003). Another publication website provides access to more than 30 reports related to territorial finance departments since 2000. Open budget data can be displayed on the screen or downloaded in PDF or XLS formats.

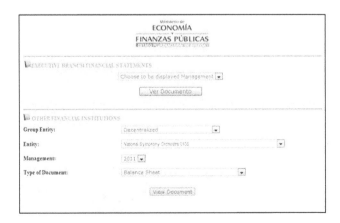

Brazil

The SIAFI portal provides a number of dynamic query options to generate open budget data in HTML or Worksheet format. The month of the last database update is shown at the upper right corner, and the report type, year, and other parameters can be selected from available options. One of the query options for generating reports on personnel expenses or other expenses and capital costs is shown at right.

Mexico

The Ministry of Finance and Public Credit/Secretaría de Hacienda y Crédito Publico (http://www.shcp.gob.mx) provides access to extensive PF data through dynamic query options. Predefined reports cover the budget performance of all public sector, federal government, and budget organizations and the social security administration. User-defined reports can be generated by selecting the type of report, period, amount to be displayed, and presentation format. Reports can be displayed online from the PF databases and downloaded in PDF or XLS formats.

Financial Management Information Systems and Open Budget Data
http://dx.doi.org/10.1596/978-1-4648-0083-2

Paraguay

The Ministry of Finance/Ministerio de Hacienda website (http://www.hacienda.gov.py) is easy to navigate and provides access to key PF information. An Online Services section includes several query options for access to state records, resource transfer requests, SIARE (the new version of the FMIS), the National System of Public Investments, Taxation, National Register, and Procurement. Query windows provide access to relevant databases, and the reports can be generated online (with download/print options).

Peru

The Ministry of Economy and Finance/Ministerio de Economía y Finanzas website presents comprehensive information about the budget performance through its Economic Transparency Portal/Portal de Transparencia Económica. A large number of dynamic query options are available to generate reports about budget execution, public and private investments, treasury operations, debt, and public accounting from the underlying FMIS. They can be displayed in various formats (XLS, Graphics, PDF).

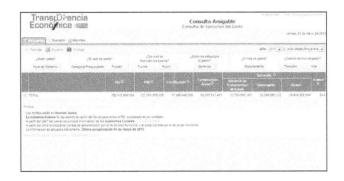

United States

The US Government launched the Open Government Initiative in 2010 to improve transparency, participation, and collaboration. The Office of Management and Budget launched USAspending.gov as a single searchable website, accessible to the public at no cost, to disclose the details of each federal contract award since 2007 (including subcontracts) and related obligations (not outlays or actual cash disbursements). The Performance.gov portal presents useful information about the performance of the government in selected areas. The US Department of the Treasury maintains a dedicated website on budget performance and publishes the Citizens Budget report.

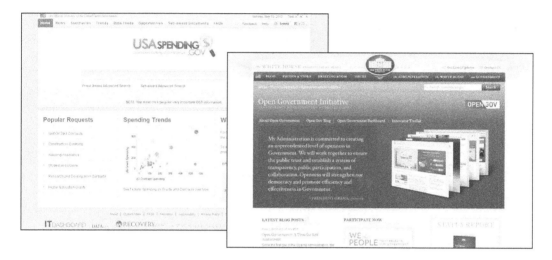

Uruguay

The Ministry of Economy and Finance (Ministerio de Economía y Finanzas) portal provides access to key PF data through interactive query options. The General Treasury of the Nation (Tesorería General de la Nación) and the General Accounting Office (Contaduría General de Nación) publish relevant details regularly. A budget execution query section can be used to generate reports online from the underlying Integrated Financial Information System (SIIF). The budgets for the current and previous periods can be analyzed in detail.

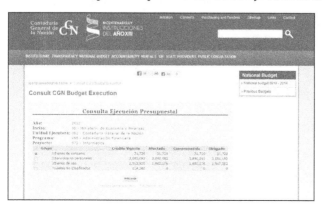

Financial Management Information Systems and Open Budget Data
http://dx.doi.org/10.1596/978-1-4648-0083-2

South Asia
India

The Data & Statistics section of the websites of the Ministry of Finance and the Controller General of Accounts present dynamic query options to create detailed reports on public finances. Selected reports are displayed as a PDF file, with a system name and date/time. Detailed reports on state loan data, expenditure statements, audit reports, national PF summary, central government borrowings, and other areas can be downloaded.

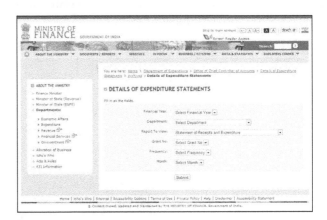

Publishing Rich Set of Open Budget Data

This section highlights several good practices in publishing a rich set of open budget data.

East Asia and Pacific
Australia

The Publications & Reports section of the Department of Finance and Deregulation website presents the key documents published in the last decade. There are well-established standards for web publishing, content management, open data, information security, ICT infrastructure, and guide to open source software, among others. Guidance for the Australian Government in publishing Public Sector Information is also available on the Open Government website (http://data.gov.au).

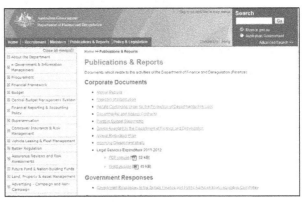

Republic of Korea

The Ministry of Strategy and Finance DBAS website provides access to a rich set of open budget data. Reports can be produced directly from the DBAS data warehouse and displayed online according to selected budget classification segments or other parameters. The download section presents a large number of display options on various operating systems in a range of formats (PDF, DOC, XLS, PPT, and so on) and languages. The budget status, consolidated results (general, central, and local budget levels), and financial indicators are updated daily and presented along with news and economic reports.

Taiwan, China

The Directorate General of Budget, Accounting and Statistics (DGBAS) website presents extensive PF information obtained from the databases of the Government Budget Accounting system. The central and special budget, as well as city and local government budgets, can be monitored in various formats (XLS, PDF) from the DGBAS website, along with relevant laws and regulations, statistics, and other economic reports.

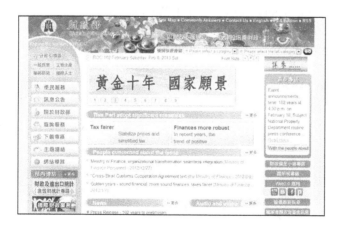

Vietnam

The Ministry of Finance website presents (http://www.mof.gov.vn) extensive open budget data about the performance of state and local budget execution from existing information systems. A new Treasury and Budget Management Information System (TABMIS) is expected to be fully operational in 2013 to support the publication of open budget data. All budget reports, investments, and final accounts are regularly updated and displayed online, and displayed results can be downloaded in XLS format.

Europe and Central Asia

Ireland

The Department of Public Expenditure and Reform initiated the Ireland Stat project in 2012 to publish open data about how public money is spent, allocated, and accounted for. The Government Performance Measurement website presents useful and meaningful performance information on three policy areas (Economy, Transport, Environment), and four more areas will be added by 2014 (Health, Education, Public Safety, Government). The pilot project sets out over 480 indicators across four categories of information (achievements, actions, costs, comparisons). Regularly updated indicators can be viewed online and exported in PDF, XLS, or DOC formats.

The Netherlands

The open data portal of the Dutch government (https://data.overheid.nl) provides information on public government data and the national Registry Open Data, with references to open data sets in government organizations. One of the open data sets is the State Budget (a summary of expenses, liabilities, and revenue by product of departmental budgets), which can be downloaded in CSV format. Other data sets provide information on education, national roads, legislation, and more. The Ministry of Finance/Ministerie van Financiën website provides access to additional open data on the state budget.

Norway

The Ministry of Finance/Finansdepartementet maintains a dedicated website for publishing comprehensive information about the performance of the State Budget/Statsbudsjettet (http://www.statsbudsjettet.no). Predefined reports can be displayed online and downloaded in several formats (HTML, PDF, XLS). In addition to detailed information about various aspects of the state budget, policy documents, government priorities, new rules and revised legislation, and press releases are posted regularly.

Financial Management Information Systems and Open Budget Data
http://dx.doi.org/10.1596/978-1-4648-0083-2

The United Kingdom

The Combined Online Information System (COINS) is the database of UK Government expenditures, managed by HM Treasury. All reports are built centrally, mainly using SQL and VBA, for output in XLS/CSV (for any period since 2005). COINS has three data streams (forecasts, budget plans/outturns, audited results) and is used for main estimates, national statistics, public expenditure statistical analyses, performance monitoring, fiscal management, ad hoc information/reports, and public accounts. Data are provided by central government departments, which retain ownership of their data on COINS.

North and South America

Brazil

The Historical Series section and other parts of the National Treasury webpages, and the Federal Budget portal, present a number of reporting options to produce a rich set of open budget data. Most of the reports can be viewed or downloaded in an editable Worksheet format. The Access to Information portal explains the procedures for access to various public sector websites and available open data. The Citizen Information Service/Serviço de Informações ao Cidadão (www.acessoainformacao.gov.br/sistema) provides access to open government data and other information.

Chile

The Budget Directorate/Dirección de Presupuestos (DIPRES) Publications website provides access to a rich set of open budget data in several formats (PDF, XLS, CSV, XML). Government financial statistics are published regularly, and key PF information on the operations of the central government and public enterprises is presented, together with budget execution updates (monthly/quarterly) and government debt. Reports are also categorized in terms of the period, institution, and content type.

Colombia

The Integrated Financial Information System/Sistema Integrado de Información Financiera (SIIF Nation) provides timely and reliable information on consolidated results of the general budget, and exercises control over the budget execution of the central government and decentralized units. A territorial assistance section includes an interactive map of all regions for easy access to relevant information.

Guatemala

The Ministry of Public Finance/Ministerio de Finanzas Públicas (http://www.minfin.gob.gt) website includes several links to important PF data portals on which open budget data from SIAF (Sistema Integrado de Administración Financiera) for the central government and municipalities are available. The Local Government Portal presents the budget performance of municipalities through an interactive map, by posting reports dynamically from the SIAF Muni database.

Reliability of PF Information Published on the Web

The examples presented in this section highlight websites that include the system name and a date/time stamp as part of ensuring the reliability of open budget data generated from FMIS.

Africa
The Gambia

The Integrated Financial Management Information System (IFMIS) was introduced by the Ministry of Finance and Economic Affairs (MoFEA) in 2007 for budget preparation, execution, accounting, and reporting (including donor-funded projects). Since 2011, the system is used by all central government entities. The IFMIS General Ledger reports include the system name and a date/time stamp. Monthly budget execution results are published on the MoFEA website.

Zambia

The Integrated Financial Management and Information System (IFMIS) is used for the preparation and execution of the state budget. Some of the budget reports include the system name and a date stamp to clarify the source of information.

System name (IFMIS) ————⟍   Date stamp ——⟍

EXPENDITURE BY HEAD ON MPSAs ON IFMIS AS AT 14/12/2012		
GRZ HEAD		Budget
Overall Result		29,609,791,800,715.70 ZMK
07	OFFICE OF THE AUDITOR GENERAL	77,732,965,545.00 ZMK
11	ZAMBIA POLICE - MINISTRY OF HOME AFFAIRS	824,720,244,968.08 ZMK
14	MINISTRY OF MINES AND MINERAL DEVELOPMEN	105,046,122,830.66 ZMK
15	MINISTRY OF HOME AFFAIRS	275,384,548,755.48 ZMK

East Asia and Pacific
Republic of Korea

The Digital Budget and Accounting System (DBAS) website provides access to extensive open budget data through dynamic query options. Although the DBAS system name and a date/time stamp are not visible on the budget documents posted, a large number of predefined reports are available for providing rapid access to reliable data from DBAS.

Thailand

The Government Financial Management Information System (GFMIS) website presents a rich set of open budget data on budget execution performance, key indicators, and other important aspects. Most of the reports generated from the system include a footer with the system name and a date/time stamp to clarify the source of information and date of publication.

Financial Management Information Systems and Open Budget Data
http://dx.doi.org/10.1596/978-1-4648-0083-2

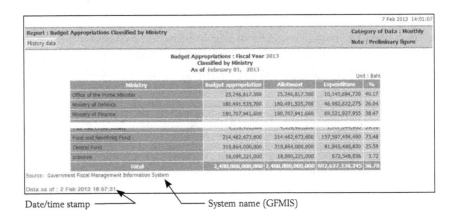

Date/time stamp ——————— ←————— System name (GFMIS)

Europe and Central Asia
Slovenia
The Ministry of Finance (Ministrstvo za finance) website provides access to key FMIS modules, the MFERAC Uniform Accounting System and SAPPrA web application for Budgeting and Analysis. Bulletins of public finances and other budget reports are generated from these systems, and they include a date/time stamp in the header section and the system name in the footer.

System name ——————— ←————— Date/time stamp

North and South America
Bolivia
The Sistema Integrado de Gestión y Modernización Administrativa (SIGMA) provides reliable information about the budget and performance management. Almost all reports include a header section with the system name indicated on the upper left corner, and a date/time stamp visible on the upper right corner. The date and time of reports from previous budget years reflect the latest publication date and remain the same, demonstrating the consistency of records generated from the system.

Brazil

The Sistema Integrado de Administração Financeira (SIAFI) is a web-based application providing reliable information from system databases through interactive query options or archived documents. The system name and a date/time stamp are visible at the top of most budget reports.

Dominican Republic

The Sistema Integrado de Gestión Financiera (SIGEF) provides timely and reliable information on budget execution. The reports published on the Ministry website include a header section with system name and date/time stamp. Other monthly statistics based on the SIGEF database are also available from the Ministry website.

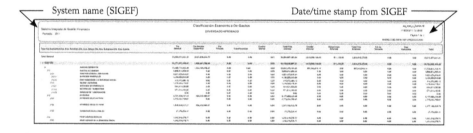

Nicaragua

The Ministry of Finance and Public Credit (Ministerio de Hacienda y Crédito Público) is using TRANSMUNI (Sistema de Transferencias Municipales) to manage transfers to municipalities from the general budget. Almost all reports published through the TRANSMUNI website include a header section with the system name and a date/time stamp.

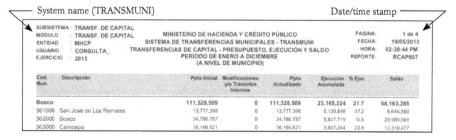

Financial Management Information Systems and Open Budget Data
http://dx.doi.org/10.1596/978-1-4648-0083-2

Middle East and North Africa
West Bank and Gaza

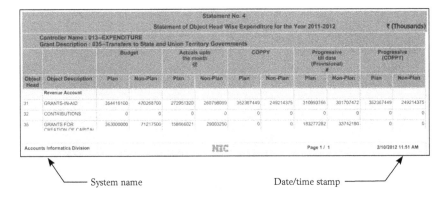

System name   Date/time stamp

The Financial Management Information System (BISAN) supports budgeting and financial management functions. The reports produced from BISAN about financial operations contain the system name and a date stamp at the bottom, together with additional explanations, to indicate the source of published data.

South Asia
India

E-Lekha supports daily reporting of expenditure in sync with the budget allocated to a ministry and its subunits. e-Lekha supports near-real-time reporting, as well as financial monitoring and control. The reports published in the ministry website include a footer section with the system name and a date/time stamp.

System name   Date/time stamp

Quality of Presentation and Interactivity

This section presents some good practice cases that demonstrate the use of innovative solutions and highly interactive websites for improving the quality of presentation of open budget data.

Financial Management Information Systems and Open Budget Data
http://dx.doi.org/10.1596/978-1-4648-0083-2

East Asia and Pacific

Australia

The Department of Finance and Deregulation has a well-maintained and informative Procurement website providing comprehensive information about all public tenders and contracts. A number of procurement guidelines are available, including specific documents designed to support ICT procurement activities. Annual procurement plans, notices, and contracts, as well as training/professional development opportunities, are updated regularly.

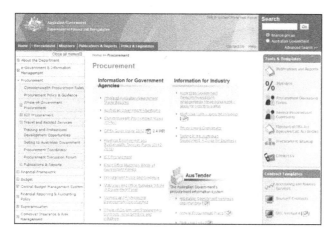

Republic of Korea

The Ministry of Strategy and Finance and Digital Budget and Accounting System (DBAS or dBrain) websites present extensive information through well-designed graphical user interfaces. A wide variety of open data display and download options are available, together with feedback mechanisms and social media links. A promotion video and other documents provide information about the dBrain modules, advanced budget performance monitoring functions, development history, lessons learned, user surveys, international cooperation, and more.

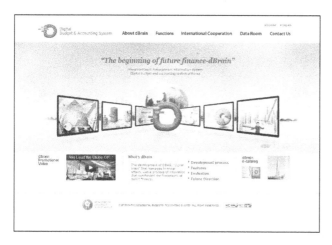

Financial Management Information Systems and Open Budget Data
http://dx.doi.org/10.1596/978-1-4648-0083-2

New Zealand

The New Zealand Treasury website provides access to extensive PF information through mobile applications and other interactive tools (Twitter, Facebook, YouTube, and so on). A new budget application (NZ Budget) was launched in December 2012 to present 2012 and 2013 budget data on mobile devices (iPad, iPhone, Android), together with budget-related videos, budget speech, executive summary, and key facts for taxpayers. A tablet version provides additional information on the Budget Economic and Fiscal Update and the Half-Year update.

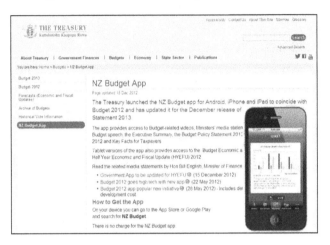

Philippines

The Government of the Philippines initiated the development of the Integrated Financial Management Information System (GIFMIS) to strengthen the public administration and improve PFM performance and service delivery. Key PFM oversight agencies (Commission on Audit, Department of Budget and Management, Department of Finance, and Bureau of the Treasury) are improving their websites and online services to support these activities. PFM-related websites were updated substantially in 2012, and several important services (Citizens Portal, Budget 101, My Budget, PFM Portal, e-Payment) are available to citizens.

Financial Management Information Systems and Open Budget Data
http://dx.doi.org/10.1596/978-1-4648-0083-2

Singapore

The Ministry of Finance maintains a highly interactive and informative budget website for publishing timely open data from the FMIS data warehouse. Each budget year is presented in separate websites with comprehensive information about budget preparation, execution, and results. Budget 2013 mobile application (iPhone, iPad) allows citizens to access the latest information about the Singapore budget, as well as press releases and announcements, videos, a budget quiz, and an e-mail subscription for the budget speech.

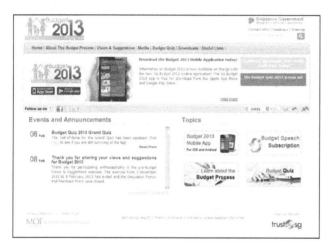

Europe and Central Asia

Austria

The Ministry of Finance (Bundesministerium für Finanzen) provides the Finance Online service through which citizens can file tax returns and request electronic notices, and companies can pay sales tax and income or corporation taxes. The Business Service Portal is another central electronic service platform for electronic billing (mandatory from January 2014) and the registration of employees using digital signatures. Links to performance-based management, Pan European Public Procurement Online, and other services provide an integrated platform for improving the quality of public service delivery.

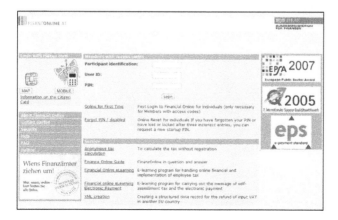

Financial Management Information Systems and Open Budget Data
http://dx.doi.org/10.1596/978-1-4648-0083-2

Finland

Suomi.fi is the Finnish public administration's one-stop service for citizens. The portal contains e-services and forms, links to relevant institutions, information packages, legislation, and news from public administration. A service map provides contact and location information for public sector services. The Citizen's Account service can be used to check the progress of an application or inquiry, send in additional information to support an application, and switch between the services of different organizations without having to register again.

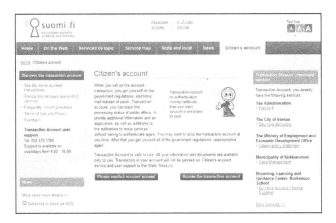

Russian Federation

The Ministry of Finance is developing e-Budget as an integrated FMIS solution to improve service delivery and transparency, following the rollout of the Federal Treasury Automation System in 2012. As a part of ongoing reforms, a mobile application (Public Services) was developed for smart phones/tablets (on Android, iOS, Windows Phone) for checking tax obligations, applying for or renewing driver's licenses, paying traffic fines, and other services. The MoF portal also provides information on reaching retirement, migration, obtaining grants and social assistance, and acquiring real estate.

Spain

The Ministry of Finance and Public Administration (Ministerio de Hacienda y Administraciones Públicas) maintains a dedicated portal for Autonomous Communities to provide information about local budgets, and access to online services. Citizens and users can log in with digital certificates to use online services. A list of all electronic services and information systems is available, together with a geomapping tool for displaying the latest data on central and local budgets.

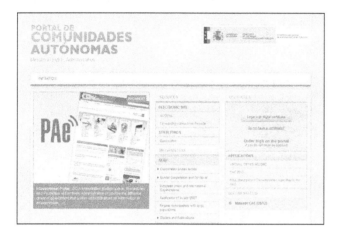

Turkey

The Public Expenditure and Accounting Information System/Kamu Harcama ve Muhasebe Bilişim Sistemi (KBS) portal was developed by the General Directorate of Public Accounts/Muhasebat Genel Müdürlüğü to provide access to key FMIS functions and online services by more than 200,000 public employees in 60,000 central and local entities. In addition to providing various expenditure management modules, the system is used to manage all personnel records and automate payroll calculations/payments.

Financial Management Information Systems and Open Budget Data
http://dx.doi.org/10.1596/978-1-4648-0083-2

North and South America
Brazil

The Comptroller General of the Union has an informative website dedicated to raising public awareness and encouraging monitoring of budget spending. The "Get Smart in Public Money/Olho Vivo no Dinheiro Público" program is designed as a learning platform for citizens to monitor the use of public resources. Local leaders, councils, local government officials, teachers, and students are informed about the importance of transparency and accountability in the public sector, and compliance with legal provisions (including a distance education option).

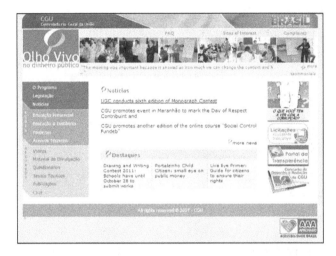

Chile

The Budget Directorate/Dirección de Presupuestos (DIPRES) maintains an easy-to-use Documents website providing access to open budget data related to public finance and economic indicators, as well as laws and regulations, presentations, speeches, and statistics. Each PF site has a specific web page on transparency, providing easy access to relevant links on access to information, regulations, procurement notices, contracts, and feedback provision mechanisms. Procurement Agency/Dirección Chile Compra also has a very informative website.

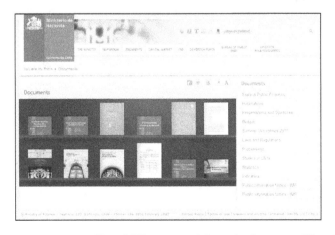

Colombia

The Fiscal Transparency Portal/Portal de Transparencia Económica presents inter-active query options (http://www.pte.gov.co) to display the budget execution performance in different sectors and provide historical data on budget programs, investments, and the medium-term budget framework. Most of the websites support open budget data in various formats (XLS, PDF, HTML). The portal includes all important web links to PF institutions for presenting additional information on procurement, debt, assets, and the details of sectoral and regional spending.

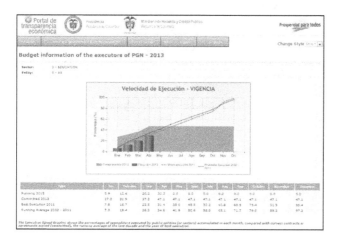

El Salvador

The Ministry of Finance/Ministerio de Hacienda presents substantial information about revenues, expenditures, investments, public debt, and procurement, as well as statistics on public finances, human resources, and foreign trade through the new Fiscal Transparency Portal. The budget monitoring section includes a snapshot of the execution rate for various institutions (plans vs. actuals) with regular updates. A large number of interactive query options are listed to generate and download desired reports as open data (XLS, PDF).

Mexico

The Ministry of Finance and Public Credit/Secretaría de Hacienda y Crédito Publico maintains a highly interactive and easy-to-navigate Budget Transparency/ Transparencia Presupuestaria portal. The portal presents detailed information about public investments, public finance, performance evaluation system, Citizens Budget, and federal agencies. Geomapping of relevant data provides useful feedback on the details of spending (who, why, where, how). The Performance Evaluation System/Sistema de Evaluación del Desempeño is available to track the performance of public policies and budget programs and verify compliance with goals and objectives. There is also a dedicated website for Financial Education/ Educación Financiera to support online learning.

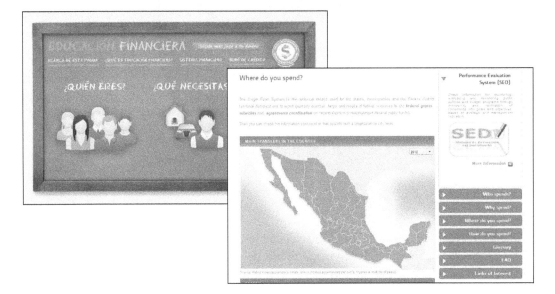

Effective Use of Open Budget Data

This section highlights government websites that present open budget data effectively so that citizens/civil society can readily monitor the performance and transparency of budget spending.

East Asia and Pacific
Republic of Korea

The Ministry of Strategy and Finance DBAS website provides extensive information about the details of budget spending. The Korean Institute of Public Finance (KIPF) developed the InfoGraphic website to present open budget data in a format that would help taxpayers understand how public money is being spent. The KIPF website presents the results of policy-oriented research on taxation, public budgeting, and state-owned enterprises across various levels of the government, and it assists the government in formulating and implementing public policies.

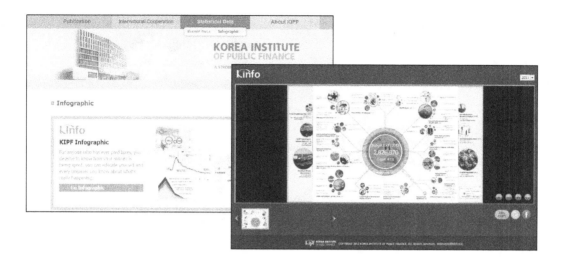

Philippines

The Public Financial Management reform website presents detailed information about ongoing activities, including accounting and auditing reforms, GIFMIS implementation, improvements in cash management through centralized treasury single account operations, and other activities. New features introduced by the Department of Budget Management (DBM) include the online submission of budget proposals. The DBM's Budget ng Bayan website presents the whole budget process and performance indicators, as well as open budget data.

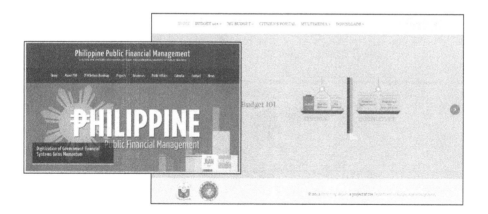

Singapore

The Ministry of Finance website presents substantial information about the Singapore Government Budget, with a clear explanation of key budget initiatives to benefit households and businesses. Citizens and civil society can share their feedback, and the MoF responds on the web, summarizing all feedback received and explaining how it was incorporated in the preparation of the new budget.

Financial Management Information Systems and Open Budget Data
http://dx.doi.org/10.1596/978-1-4648-0083-2

Video highlights and relevant budget documents/speeches provide useful additional feedback on budget planning/execution process.

Europe and Central Asia
Germany
The Ministry of Finance/Bundesministerium der Finanzen provides access to federal budget information through websites, social media, and mobile applications. The interactive website presenting the Federal Budget/Bundeshaushalt (http://www.bundeshaushalt-info.de) revenues and expenditures (according to budget sections, functional category, and the spending groups of all government institutions) demonstrates good practice. Results are displayed both graphically and in tabulated form, and can be downloaded as open budget data (PDF, XLS).

Financial Management Information Systems and Open Budget Data
http://dx.doi.org/10.1596/978-1-4648-0083-2

Offener Haushalt is a noncommercial project designed to visualize, analyze, and comment on the federal and local budgets, using data available from the Federal Ministry of Finance website and other relevant sources.

Norway

The Directorate for Financial Management (DFØ) maintains an easy-to-navigate and innovative portal to provide core PFM services for government agencies through shared platforms. DFØ is responsible for managing national accounts and for maintaining the standard CoA, accounting standards, and the government's cash. The DFØ manages payroll, accounting, e-Commerce, e-Invoice, and other services, and the operational status of all systems (Agresso, EFB, SAP, Integration Engine) can be monitored online. DFØ also organizes forums for the exchange of experiences and disseminates good practice through professional networks.

To provide meaningful information on public finances, the Ministry of Finance has developed a web portal (http://www.ungokonomi.no) that is easy for citizens and civil society organizations to understand and navigate. It provides regular updates on economics and budget issues.

Russian Federation

The Ministry of Finance maintains a website for regular updates on key performance indicators about the budget system. Budget data (federal and consolidated), macroeconomic indicators, and government programs are presented through graphs/charts, and can be downloaded in PDF or XLS formats. The Federal Treasury has developed a useful data-mart system to monitor and publish key indicators related to budget execution. Another important web platform is the procurement portal, where all procurement notices, contracts, and suppliers related to federal and local-level tenders are posted and updated regularly. A new budget portal was launched in early 2013 (www.budget.gov.ru—test version) to publish a rich set of open budget data on federal and regional revenues and expenditures, investments, intergovernmental transfers, procurement activities, and more. There is a discussion forum through which citizens and civil society can provide feedback on possible improvements.

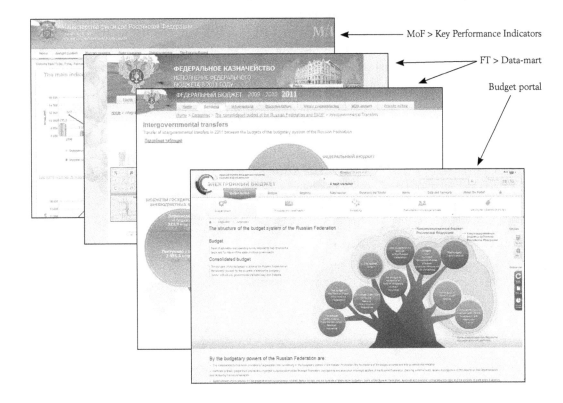

MoF > Key Performance Indicators

FT > Data-mart

Budget portal

Turkey

The General Directorate of Public Accounts of the Ministry of Finance provides access to extensive PF information based on FMIS (say2000i and KBS) databases. In addition to secure access to KBS, automated payroll calculations (e-Bordro), revolving funds, and statistics, the portal presents service quality standards, regulations, and the latest news. Regular updates on local administration budgets and other important indicators are published as graphics and open budget data (XLS, PDF).

A civil society website was launched in 2010 (Public Expenditures Monitoring Platform/Kamu Harcamalarını İzleme Platformu) to monitor public expenditures and send reports to the parliament about possible improvements in public spending allocations/priorities and policy, based on the budget plans and actual spending data published on the MoF websites.

The United Kingdom

"Where Does My Money Go?" was launched in 2007 to promote citizen engagement and transparency through analysis and visualization of data about UK public spending. This project, expanded as the "Open Spending" initiative, now includes 212 PF data sets from 53 economies. The graphical user interface explains how tax revenues are divided among the different units, and how much is spent for various functions in total and where. A Country & Regional Analysis section includes links to similar transparency websites.

North and South America
Argentina

The Ministry of Economy and Public Finance maintains a website for citizens and civil society to improve the transparency of public management. Key information about the execution of the national budget is presented in simple language. Citizens can also access budget data through charts, graphs, and tables for additional details on budget revenues and expenditures, and for comparison with previous periods. Dynamic query options are available to generate selected reports online, with a system date/time stamp and user-friendly presentations. A survey form is also included for receiving feedback from visitors.

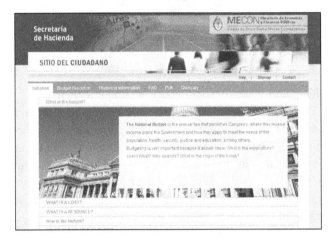

Dominican Republic

The Citizens Portal/Portal del Ciudadano (http://www.portaldelciudadano.gov.do) presents comprehensive information about the execution of the budget based on SIGFE databases and benefiting from business intelligence queries. A number of quick access queries are available: What is spent? Who spends? How is it spent? and Where is it spent? Links to relevant public institutions are included, along with feedback provision forms. Most of the reports are generated (and can be reproduced) from the SIGEF databases with a clear indication of the system name and a date/time stamp.

Brazil

The Brazilian Transparency Portal/Portal da Transparência is one of the fine examples of presenting meaningful PF information to citizens and civil society organizations. It provides a number of dynamic query options on all important aspects, and includes links to other government portals: Federal Budget, National Treasury, Public Accounts, the procurement portal, the Planning and Management Information System, the transparency portal of the Chamber of Deputies, constitutional transfers, and more.

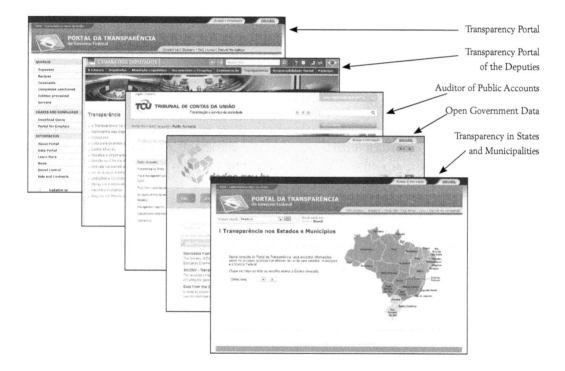

Transparency Portal

Transparency Portal of the Deputies

Auditor of Public Accounts

Open Government Data

Transparency in States and Municipalities

Mexico

The Budget Transparency/Transparencia Presupuestaria portal of the Ministry of Finance and Public Credit uses the Citizens Budget to share meaningful information about budget spending, investments, public sector salaries, and other reference documents. Previous Citizens Budget reports are also available (since 2010) in PDF. Citizens Budget 2013 is also available as an iPad application. The Investment section uses interactive maps to present the annual distribution of budget to programs/projects of the federal portfolio by executing unit or by state.

Financial Management Information Systems and Open Budget Data
http://dx.doi.org/10.1596/978-1-4648-0083-2

FMIS World Map

One of the important outputs of this study is the development of the FMIS
World Map, which provides access to the web links (URLs) of PF websites in 198
economies, as well as 176 FMIS supporting key PFM operations in these countries. The FMIS World Map is a geospatial mapping application developed on
Google Maps; it benefits from free open-source data conversion software (XLS
to KML) and a free public mapping option provided by Google. Icons with a
letter (A to D) are used as place marks (on capital cities) to reflect the FMIS &
OBD group of 198 government websites.

When a user selects one of the icons on the map, the following basic information
is displayed, along with any Open Government/Open Data web link (Map 4.1).

Country Name ... FMIS abbreviation		[Functional scope: F/T]
Location	:	Capital city [Income level]
System	:	Full name of the FMIS solution in native language
Group	:	A - D *[FMIS & OBD practices]*
Status	:	FMIS operational status [Since: year]
Web links	:	FMIS, Finance Ministry/Dept, Central Bank, Statistics, and Open Gov/Open Data URLs.

The Beta version of the FMIS World Map was developed in June 2012 and updated several times before the completion of this study in June 2013. The FMIS World Map will be updated annually to improve the visibility of the findings, and to provide easy and open public access to good practices (Map 4.2).

Map 4.1 Basic information and web links displayed on FMIS World Map

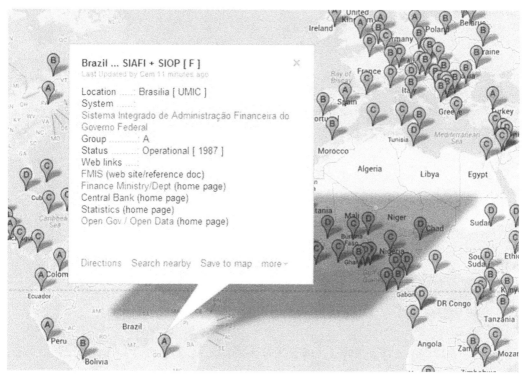

Source: World Bank data.

Map 4.2 FMIS World Map (as of June 2013)

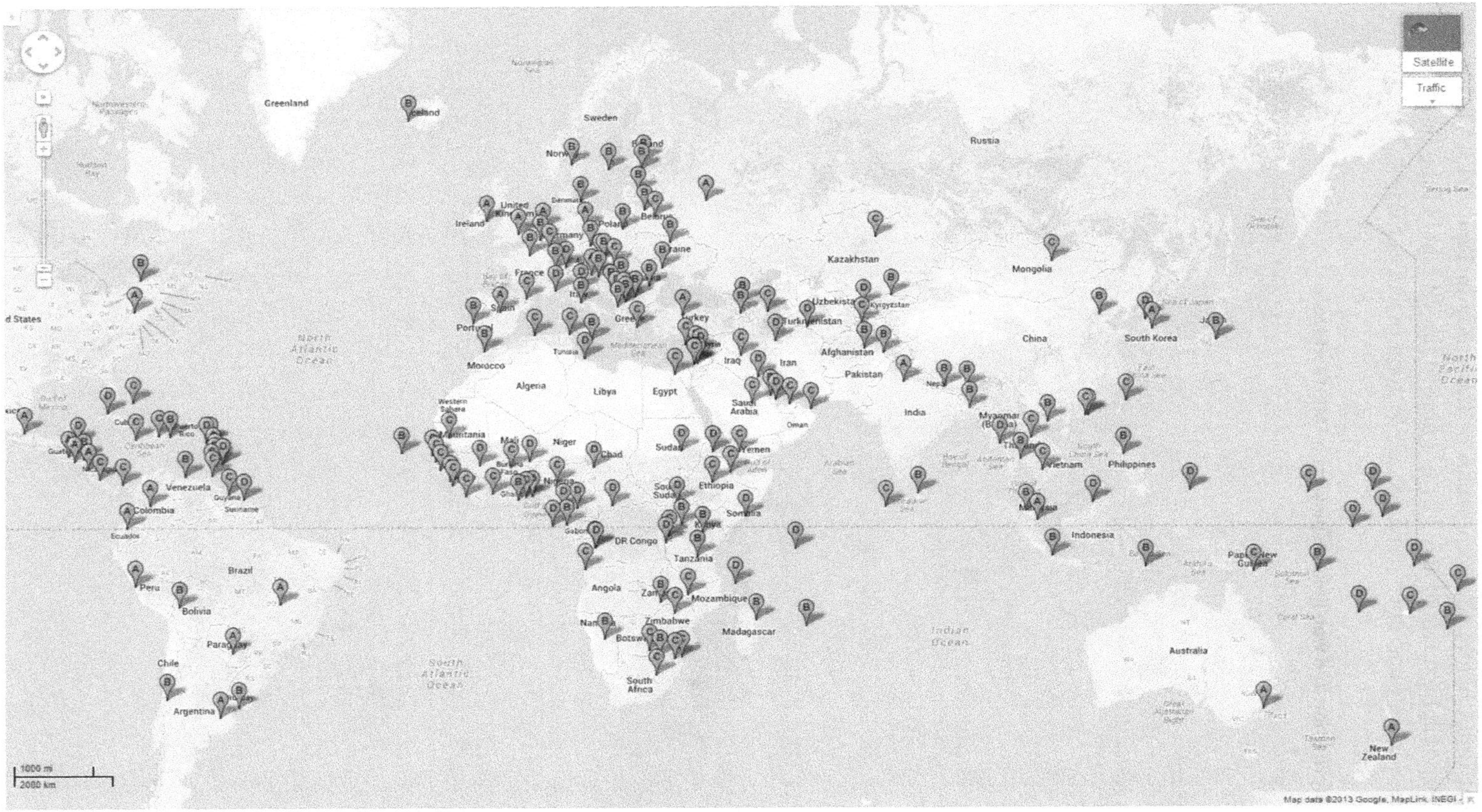

Source: FMIS World Map.
http://maps.google.com/maps/ms?ie=UTF&msa=0&msid=213542822110887565899.0004c2f44512d9ce6795f

Note

1. The DBAS/dBrain (IFMIS solution of the Ministry of Strategy and Finance of the Republic of Korea) is the winner (first place in Category 4, EAP region) of the 2012 United Nations Public Service Awards (UNPSA) for promoting the whole-of-government approach.

CHAPTER 5

Guidelines for Publishing Open Budget Data

Governments' interest in posting open budget data on their websites has been growing over the last decade, largely because citizens and civil society groups are increasingly demanding information with which to monitor the details of public revenues, expenditures, and debt, as well as the results of government spending and investments. Although some governments have improved the timeliness, quality, and scope of their public finance (PF) reporting, most do not pay enough attention to some of the basic principles for publishing meaningful budget data that can be downloaded, analyzed, and evaluated by citizens and civil society, and for ensuring the source and reliability of the information they publish. Guidance on publishing reliable open budget data from underlying financial management information systems (FMIS) solutions is scarce.

These guidelines, prepared to help fill this gap, have three main purposes:

- To assist *governments* in understanding the key principles for posting reliable open budget data from underlying FMIS solutions when they are developing new PF websites/portals, or improving the contents, functionality, format, or presentation quality of existing websites
- To help *civil society organizations* learn more about effective monitoring of the budget planning and implementation process and the performance of the government; and to expose them to other country experiences that they can use to improve citizen participation in their own countries
- To assist *oversight agencies* in strengthening their ability to perform their internal/external oversight role during budget implementation by ensuring that the PF information presented is reliable, and that transaction-based evidence is available from underlying information systems for consistent reporting.

The guiding principles for posting reliable open budget data are summarized below:

- Availability of timely and comprehensive budget information
- Disclosure of details about underlying information systems

- Availability of user-defined (dynamic) query and reporting capabilities
- Publication of reliable and interlinked open budget data
- Authentication of the sources of public finance data
- Improving the quality of presentation
- Promoting the effective use of open budget data.

The discussion of each of these principles in this chapter can be supplemented by reference to some of the good practice cases. The FMIS & Open Budget Data (OBD) data set and the FMIS World Map present evidence to assist in the comparison of similar practices across countries.

Availability of Timely and Comprehensive Budget Information

The design of official websites dedicated to the publication of PF information should take into account the following factors:

- *Existence of dedicated websites for access to PF data.* Frequent changes in the uniform resource locator (URL) of PF websites should be avoided. When changes are necessary (for example, because of organizational restructuring, or the merging of two institutions), relevant web links should be maintained for a while with clear explanations, to ensure the continuity of reference URLs.
- *Timely and regular publication of budget plans and execution results.* A website can be created to present the publication schedule (name, update frequency, publisher, and so on) of key PF documents. Budget plans, execution reports, and other reports should then be posted on the designated websites according to announced schedules (for example, weekly or monthly). Governments should also have in place clear procedures for updating and archiving the budget data.
- *Completeness of published PF information.* Detailed PF information should be posted during the budget year to provide a comprehensive, updated picture of the government's financial activities, as well as those of state/local governments, when applicable. (See key budget documents suggested in the Open Budget Survey.) The IMF Data Quality Assessment Framework for Government Finance Statistics is a useful guideline that comprehensively covers the quality aspects of data collection, processing, and dissemination.[1]
- *Presentation of budget execution performance through time-series data.* Access to online budget archives presenting the policies, PF information, and major achievements should be provided to facilitate comparative analysis and observation of the variations in transparency and accountability over time.

Disclosure of Details About Underlying Information Systems

The dedicated websites should explain key aspects of the PFM information systems, along with important functional/technical capabilities, standards, and policies.

- *Presenting the key features of underlying information systems*. The website should contain adequate details about the functionality, operational status, technical architecture, scope, number of users, and other important aspects of the underlying information systems (FMIS, data warehouse [DW], or other).
- *Promoting the use of interoperability standards and digital signature*. The government's interoperability standards—policies and specifications governing the use of ICT in the government, as well as the rules/formats of interaction among government entities—need to be defined clearly on the dedicated website. Public finance management (PFM) operations should use a digital signature as part of ensuring the quality and reliability of the services delivered.
- *Disclosure of data protection and information security policies*. For the best-managed PFM information systems, relevant publications or FMIS websites should clearly describe the government's data protection and information security policy and practices. The requirements to protect the confidentiality of personal or classified information should be considered while posting open data.

Availability of User-defined (Dynamic) Query and Reporting Capabilities

User-defined (dynamic) query tools developed on FMIS databases or DW solutions are becoming standard features of integrated PFM systems.

- *Capability to analyze multidimensional data interactively*. Integrated FMIS solutions should be designed to link operational systems (OLTP—supporting online transaction processing and preserving data integrity, with minimal back-end reporting options) with powerful DW solutions (OLAP—supporting online high-volume analytical processing and elaborate report generation) to provide interactive query options to analyze multidimensional data from different perspectives. The update frequency of key databases should be displayed in dynamic query websites to clarify the refresh schedules.
- *Flexible and user-friendly dynamic query, reporting, and download options*. Interactive query and reporting platforms linked with the underlying FMIS database or DW are ideal for presenting relevant information according to user preferences. Query results can be displayed online in various forms (graphics, charts, tables, text) or downloaded in desired open data formats (for example, XML, CSV, XLS, ODF, DOC) to support internal and external reporting needs.
- *Consistency of historical data*. It should be possible to reproduce the government financial statistics or other official reports of previous budget years by extracting historical data from integrated FMIS or DW solutions, as a verification of the integrity and reliability of underlying databases. Separate presentation of historical data (frozen) and operational reports (regularly updated during the budget year), and proper explanations about the stability and consistency of the data presented, also help in the interpretation of posted results.

Financial Management Information Systems and Open Budget Data
http://dx.doi.org/10.1596/978-1-4648-0083-2

Publication of Reliable and Interlinked Open Budget Data

Publishing open budget data (free, online, editable) from DW solutions linked with FMIS databases is very important to improve the accuracy and reusability of PF data.

- *Publishing open budget data on the web requires a cultural change*. Posting open budget data requires a change in the mindsets of politicians and government officials, who must be committed to increasing public confidence by allowing more visibility into operations. This is both an adaptive and a technical challenge for PF officials and ICT specialists, who should manage this change effectively to ensure that their motivations are properly understood and supported.
- *Benefiting from the guidelines on publishing open data*. A number of guidelines define the minimum requirements and web publishing standards for open government data—for example, Australia, Brazil, New Zealand, EU Public Sector Information Platform, and The World Bank Open Data. The World Wide Web Consortium has developed specific guidelines to help governments open and share their data, emphasizing the importance of metadata to clarify the structure of posted data and related standards (for example, Resource Description Framework, or RDF).

   The World Bank released the Open Government Data Toolkit in 2012, to provide staff and government officials a basic set of resources for initiating and developing an open data program. The toolkit includes five components: (a) Open Data Essentials; (b) Technology Options; (c) Demand and Engagement; (d) Supply and Quality of Data; and (e) Readiness Assessment Tool. Another useful reference is the Open Data Handbook, which presents the legal, social, and technical aspects of open data. These resources can very helpful during the development of open budget data portals.
- *Open budget data creates opportunities to add value to public information.* As a part of FMIS modernization efforts, some governments are publishing open budget data to provide opportunities for new products and improved service delivery by adding value to PF data, which is difficult and expensive to capture. PF websites should provide multiple access options, including full downloads and Application Programming Interface (API) for developers.
- *Paying attention to the legal aspects of open government data.* Open data should ideally be license-free (that is, not subject to any copyright, patent, or trademark). However, reasonable privacy, security, and privilege restrictions may be acceptable. The legal aspects of open budget data should be clarified on government websites, either by using existing licensing/legal options (for example, Creative Commons licenses) or by defining country-specific legal requirements. Existing open data licensing options include (a) Public domain (no rights reserved: CCo); (b) Attribution (credit must be given: CC-BY); and (c) Sharealike (data should be shared back: CC-BY-SA).

Authentication of the Sources of Public Finance Data

Visibility of a system name and a date/time stamp on published reports is one of the key indicators for the reliability and integrity of underlying information systems.

- *Displaying system name and date/time stamp on official reports.* The source of information should be clearly visible on all official reports/publications posted on PF data websites. In addition to the system name and the date/time stamp of generated reports, the version of the related FMIS should also be visible.
- *Safeguards to protect information from unauthorized modification or access.* The integrity of PF information should be ensured by implementing appropriate safeguards to protect data from unauthorized modification and access. Also, the availability of information should be secured by preventing the denial of authorized access. Privileged access rights should also be monitored by the information and communication technology (ICT) risk and compliance units. Moreover, necessary oversight mechanisms should be in place to ensure the reliability and integrity of databases, the security of operations, and the effectiveness of information technology (IT) governance and oversight functions.

Improving the Quality of Presentation

Interactive data visualization options, graphical user interfaces, feedback mechanisms, and advanced search/reporting options substantially improve the quality of presentation in PF websites.

- *Creating searchable interactive maps of PF information.* Interactive maps are very useful to present the details of PF information in a user-friendly format (for example, sectors, regions, gender focus, programs/activities). A number of visualization platforms are available (including open source software and free public versions of visualization packages) to rapidly post key PF data on searchable interactive maps (for example, Knoema, Tableau, RapidMiner, Ushahidi).
- *Broadening access to PF data through mobile applications.* Governments are increasingly sharing financial activities with citizens through mobile devices (tablets/smart phones). Some of the advanced applications provide online payment and search options as well.
- *Providing daily updates on key performance indicators.* Advanced applications for data marts (subsets of data stored in a warehouse) can support daily updates on critical PF information. DWs should be updated regularly (often daily) from the operational systems (FMIS databases) to support the timely presentation of selected indicators through data marts (see Figure 5.1).

Financial Management Information Systems and Open Budget Data
http://dx.doi.org/10.1596/978-1-4648-0083-2

Figure 5.1 Publishing timely and reliable open budget data from FMIS solutions

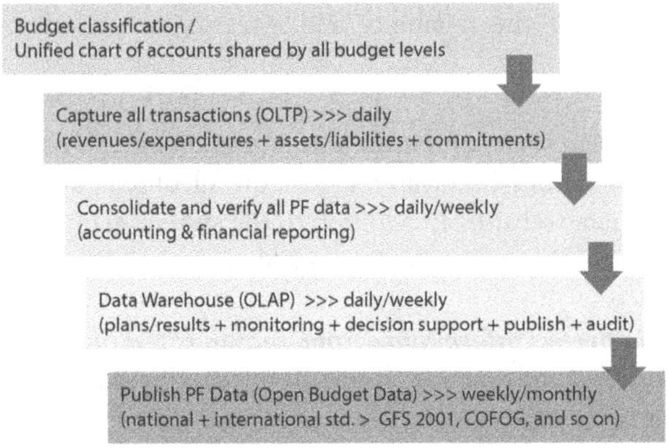

Source: World bank data
Note: OLTP = Online Transaction Processing; OLAP = Online Analytical Processing; PF = Public Finance; GFS = Government Finance Statistics; COFOG = Classification of the Functions of Government.

Promoting the Effective Use of Open Budget Data

Publishing meaningful open data on budget revenues, spending, and other financial activities is crucial for any government to explain how public money has been spent. The Citizens Budget is an important instrument to achieve this.

- *Measuring the government's financial performance.* Governments should regularly publish on the web the supreme audit institution's audit reports on the financial performance of the government in the previous budget year. Oversight agencies should have read-only access to FMIS databases, linked with DW solutions, so that they can dynamically monitor and audit the budget execution performance.
- *Availability of the Citizens Budget and feedback mechanisms.* A Citizens Budget is a website or document that explains basic budget information using simple and clear language. Using a regularly updated website to present the Citizens Budget is an important indicator of the government's commitment to improving budget transparency and participation. The International Budget Partnership (IBP) has published a guide on Citizens Budgets ("The Power of Making It Simple," May 2012), offering useful tips to governments interested in developing a Citizens Budget. The Citizens Budget should be prepared in consultation with citizens about what they would like to know about the budget. Feedback provided by the citizens and relevant adjustments should be posted on the Citizens Budget websites to complement the publication of meaningful open budget data.
- *Promoting public consultation and participation in the budget process.* Participatory budgeting is a process (different from the Citizens Budget) through which people in a locality or community can participate in budget decision making and affect the government's budget. The publication of open budget

data should be complemented by engaging the public in policy making and monitoring. Detailed discussions about public participation/engagement are offered in "The Core Principles for Public Engagement"[2] and "Deliberative Public Engagement: Nine Principles."[3]

- *Monitoring budget implementation through timely information.* Civil society groups play an important role in monitoring and analyzing the government's budget on the basis of the information available in PF websites, and publishing reports in simplified forms to enable citizens to understand what the government is doing with their money. As the IBP's guide on Citizens Budgets explains, in recent years a few governments have taken a similar task upon themselves—for example, El Salvador, Ghana, India, New Zealand, and South Africa. Recently, new budget portals have been launched (for example, Russian Federation) to present substantial information on key performance indicators with daily updates. To improve the monitoring of budget implementation, governments should make meaningful open data available to citizens and civil society groups, with timely updates (daily/weekly).
- *Demonstrating meaningful results.* The implementation status of government policies and plans should be presented clearly, together with the results of operations, to increase the transparency of government actions. In addition, the results of participatory budgeting, gender focus, or citizen-led expenditure monitoring should be published to demonstrate meaningful results.

Notes

1. The guideline can be found on http://dsbb.imf.org/images/pdfs/dqrs_gfs.pdf.
2. http://ncdd.org/rc/wp-content/uploads/2010/08/PEPfinal-expanded.pdf.
3. http://www.involve.org.uk/wp-content/uploads/2011/03/Deliberative-public-engagement-nine-principles.pdf.

CHAPTER 6

Conclusions

What You See Is (Not Always) What You Get

The average score for the performance of 198 governments in publishing open budget data from financial management information system (FMIS) is 45.1 out of 100, based on 20 key indicators. About 93 websites that present extensive or significant information appear to be benefiting from underlying information systems while publishing public finance (PF) data, but most of them do not yet provide open data.

Overall, only 48 countries (24 %) offer PF information well enough that civil society and citizens can rely on it to monitor the budget and hold the governments accountable. Also, in many countries the internal/external oversight agencies do not appear to be using the FMIS platforms effectively while monitoring the government's financial activities or auditing the budget results.

The findings of this study indicate that developing robust FMIS solutions as the source of reliable open budget data and measuring the effects of FMIS on budget transparency continue to be major challenges in many countries. This chapter summarizes the findings and conclusions of the study.

Findings

The following research questions were addressed during this exercise:

---

1. What are the important characteristics of current government web publishing platforms designed for the disclosure of budget data?

By analyzing data collected through 40 indicators, the team found that web publishing practices vary significantly among countries in different regions of the World Bank and at different income levels.

▶ The status of 198 government web publishing platforms around the world is as follows:
  - 24 governments (12 %) follow most of the good practices for publishing open budget data from reliable FMIS solutions.
  - 69 governments (35 %) provide significant budget information, but only a small portion of these publications qualify as open budget data from FMIS.
  - 60 governments (30 %) provide some information in their PF websites, mostly from archived documents without enough evidence on the use of FMIS databases as the source of published PF data.
  - 45 governments (23 %) post minimal or no budget information on the web.

▶ **Indicator 1:** Most of the governments (166 out of 198, or 83.8 %) have dedicated websites to publish PF information, and 125 of these (63.1 %) include a link to budget data clearly visible from their home pages.

▶ **Indicator 2:** About half of the governments (92 out of 198, or 46.5 %) have dedicated websites providing useful information about the functionality and current status of FMIS platforms. Also, 83 governments publish some reports about FMIS functionality/scope, but 23 present no information about FMIS.

▶ **Indicator 3:** Only 34 governments (17.2 %) have dynamic websites, and 12 of these provide access to extensive information through interactive queries, mostly linked with FMIS. A large number of countries (132 or 66.7 %) maintain static websites presenting various documents from unidentified sources.

▶ **Indicator 4:** Open budget data are visible in 52 economies (26.3 %), but only about half of these appear to be linked with FMIS databases.

▶ **Indicator 5:** Only 18 governments (9.1 %) include the name of FMIS solution as the source of published information in budget reports.

▶ **Indicator 6:** Only 28 governments (14.1 %) present PF data with a system time stamp as an evidence of direct dynamic links to underlying databases in budget reports.

▶ **Indicator 7:** 69 governments (34.8 %) provide comprehensive information about budget performance in easy-to-understand formats. The quality of reporting in a large portion of PF websites (49 %) is partially acceptable, but 32 websites (16.2 %) show little or no attention to presentation quality.

▶ **Indicator 8:** Regarding the general level of detail in budget execution reports, 148 economies (74.7 %) provide substantial data on various aspects, while the remaining 50 provide minimal or no information about the contents of publications.

▶ **Indicator 9:** Only 15 governments (7.6 %) provide interactive Citizens Budget websites through which citizens can gain access to meaningful budget data and provide feedback, and 33 governments (16.7 %) present useful information for the citizens only on budget spending. Most of the governments (75.7 %) do not provide meaningful budget information to their citizens.

▶ **Indicator 10:** 93 governments (47 %) provide Budget classification (BC)/ Chart of Accounts (CoA) details on their websites.

▶ **Indicators 11 and 12:** 153 governments (77.3 %) publish their approved annual budgets on the PF websites, and 120 of them do so regularly (at least within the last five years).

▶ **Indicators 13 and 14:** 103 governments (52 %) publish their multiyear plans or MTEF, and 64 of them regularly update their plans (revising them every year, at least within the last five years).

▶ **Indicators 15 and 16:** Only 44 governments (22.2 %) publish public investment plans separately from their annual or multiyear plans, and 32 do so regularly.

▶ **Indicators 17 and 18:** 147 governments (74.2 %) publish budget execution results at various intervals, and 117 do so regularly.

▶ **Indicators 19 and 20:** 75 governments (37.9 %) publish some reports on external audit websites about budget execution performance, and 60 of them do so regularly.

---

2. Is there any evidence on the reliability of open budget data published from FMIS?

The evidence from the first 10 key indicators shows that although the 198 economies use 176 FMIS solutions, many governments do not have comprehensive web publishing platforms to present reliable open budget data. Good practices for the publication of open budget data from reliable FMIS solutions are highly visible in only about 24 government websites (12 %).

---

3. Are there good practices demonstrating how open budget data from FMIS can improve budget transparency?

There are some good practice examples of governments that present budget results in a meaningful way so that the citizens can understand where the money goes. All of these economies have dedicated websites presenting the Citizens Budget with regular updates. Some of them also present evidence about public consultations and participatory budgeting. Several publish the results of public consultation and relevant changes in the PF policy and planned investments. Some post the results of participatory budgeting, gender focus, or citizen-led expenditure monitoring, together with interactive monitoring options. Chapter 4 presents selected good practice cases and innovative solutions.

---

4. Why is a "single version of the truth" difficult to achieve in the budget domain?

In the ICT world, the "single version of the truth" (SVOT) is a technical concept describing the data warehousing ideal of having either a single centralized database or at least a distributed synchronized database, that stores all of an organization's data in a consistent and nonredundant form. Similarly, "single source of the truth" (SSOT) refers to the practice of structuring information models such that every data element is stored exactly once. In the PF/budget domain, these ideals are difficult to achieve, since the public finance management (PFM) operational systems and data warehouses are so fragmented and widely dispersed that it is very difficult to determine the most accurate version of the PF information at a specific point in time (except frozen historical data stored in data warehouses) (Figure 6.1).

Some of the main challenges in capturing reliable open budget data are as follows:

- Difficulties in developing unified BC/CoA data structures supporting the needs of all public sector entities
- Defining BC/CoA segments in sufficient detail (optimization) to be able to record and report all economic activities with adequate disaggregation (capturing program/activity and sector/regional spending)
- Capturing all PF transactions daily, and consolidating the results weekly/ monthly for accounting and monitoring needs
- Converting country-specific PF data into IMF Government Finance Statistics (GFS), Classification of the Functions of Government (COFOG), or other internationally accepted reporting formats (bridge tables) consistently

Figure 6.1 Source and scope of public finance data

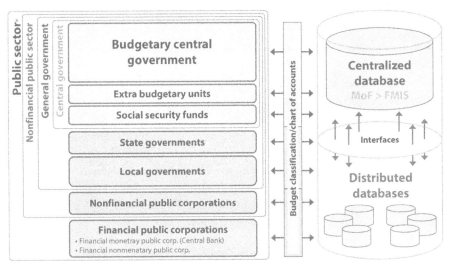

* Institutional structure of "public sector," as defined in the
IMF government finance statistics 2001 manual

Source: World Bank data.
Note: MoF = Ministry of Finance; FMIS = Financial Management Information System.

- Developing the necessary legal and regulatory framework to define the roles and responsibilities in capturing and publishing PF data on the web
- Establishing the necessary oversight mechanisms to ensure the integrity and reliability of the FMIS databases used for publishing PF information.

For complex systems, Master Data Management (MDM) can provide some practical solutions to improve consistency and control. When new systems are being developed or complete FMIS infrastructure and databases are being modernized, it may be possible to achieve SVOT with careful design and by using some industry standards.

If FMIS solutions can be effectively used to capture all transactions daily (at least at the central government level), and if related data warehouses can be updated from operational systems regularly (ideally every day), it may be possible to come close to SVOT through integrated systems. Some of the advanced FMIS solutions have data warehouse components that operate very close to this ideal.

---

5. Can there be some guidelines to improve the practices in publishing reliable open budget data from FMIS?

Using the findings of this study and the experience gained in the development of FMIS solutions funded by the World Bank in 60 countries since the 1980s, the team proposed several guiding principles (chapter 5) that should help governments, citizens/civil society groups, and oversight agencies improve their practices in publishing reliable open budget data from FMIS.

The main findings of this study are based on the rapid assessment of 198 PF websites, mostly at the central government level. However, it is important to note that there are a number of PF publication platforms at state, district, or local government levels in more than 30 economies that have fiscal decentralization and state-/agency-level FMIS solutions (for example, Brazil, Canada, India, Italy, the United States). At these subnational levels, as well, there are a number of good practices in promoting transparency and participatory budgeting.

To verify whether the findings of the study are consistent with key observations from other fiscal transparency indices, the distribution of FMIS & Open budget data (OBD) scores was compared with several relevant fiscal transparency instruments such as Public Expenditure and Financial Accountability (PEFA), Open Budget Index (OBI), and UN e-Government Development Rankings. It was found that the patterns are largely similar, and the FMIS & OBD scores correlate positively with the Public expenditure and financial accountability (PEFA) indicators and OBI scores.

Concluding Remarks

So, can we see where the money goes? The study shows that many governments publish substantial budget information on their PF websites, but the contents are (not always) meaningful to answer the question, "Where does the money go?" Only a few countries provide citizens, civil society groups, and oversight agencies with access to reliable open budget data from underlying FMIS solutions. Therefore, the main conclusion of this study is that **what you see is (not always) what you get**. Additional efforts are needed in many economies for building confidence in the budget data disclosed by the governments. However, there is rising demand from citizens and civil society for access to open government data about all financial activities, and many governments around the world are trying to respond to this democratic pressure.

Widespread use of the Internet and web technologies is transforming public sector management in many economies. Any country—regardless of income level, geographic location, or infrastructure constraints—can follow good practices in budget transparency if the government is committed to publishing open budget data from reliable FMIS databases (technology or capacity is not the main barrier). Effective budget monitoring mechanisms that benefit from existing FMIS platforms may contribute substantially to the improvement of budget transparency.

> Selected cases demonstrate that, even in difficult settings, innovative solutions to improve budget transparency can be developed rapidly, with a modest investment, if there is political will and commitment from the government.

The outputs of this study (key findings and conclusions, updated FMIS & OBD data set, selected good practices, guidelines on publishing open budget data from FMIS, and the FMIS World Map) are expected to provide a comprehensive view of the current status of government practices around the world, and to promote debates about the improvement of government PF web publishing platforms for disclosing reliable and complete information about all financial activities to support transparency, accountability, and participation.

This study is not designed to address other challenges related to the collection and disclosure of timely and reliable PF information about off-budget fiscal and quasi-fiscal activities and contingent liabilities; analyze the contents of the published PF information in detail; or reach citizens and civil society groups around the world to learn more about user perceptions and the level of utilization of open budget data by various stakeholders. These important aspects can be explored in future studies.

Explanation for Indicators/Questions and Response Options

To assess the effects of open budget data (published from financial management information systems (FMIS) solutions) on budget transparency, 40 indicators were defined in two categories:

1. *Key indicators:* 20 indicators from 10 factual questions about the source, scope, and reliability of open budget data.
2. *Informative indicators:* 20 indicators from 10 questions providing useful information about other important features.

The *key indicators* are presented below, with a brief explanation about the measurement method, points, and evidence (links/uniform resource locator (URL) of relevant web pages) of observed characteristics. The *informative indicators* and related questions follow the key indicators.

Table A.1 Key indicators

Questions	#	Indicators	Point	Response options
Q1. Does the Finance Ministry/Department have a website or portal that is dedicated to publishing public finance (PF) information?	Q1.1	PF home page Uniform Resource Locator (**URL**)		http:.........
	Q1.2	Official name of the Finance Ministry/Department		Official name of the Ministry/Dept
	Q1.3	**Is there a dedicated website for publishing PF information?**	0 1 2	No Yes (not clearly visible from home page) Yes (easy access from home page)
	Q1.4	If Yes to Q1.3 (1 or 2) > PF publication web link/URL		http:.........

Indicator 1 **Dedicated public finance publication website**

Approach: The following approach was used to locate the dedicated websites of the public finance organizations and open budget data:

a) The Finance Ministry/Department home sites were checked first to see if all questions can be answered from one source.

b) In case some of the public finance information was not visible in the MoF websites (for example, investment plans, audit reports, procurement, other websites were visited, depending on the roles/responsibilities of related organizations (for example, Ministry of Economy, Planning).

c) In addition to the MoF, Statistics, and Central Bank websites, other ministry/agency web pages (for example, Treasury, Open Budget portal) were visited to capture remaining questions.

Evidence: The URLs of relevant websites (Q1.1 and Q1.4), as well as the official name of the key PF organization (Q1.2).

Point: 2 = There is a dedicated PF website, and links to budget related information/reports are clearly visible from the home page.

1 = PF information links are not clearly visible from the home page, or are posted on separate websites without linkages to the PF home page.

0 = No dedicated website for publishing PF information is visible.

Questions	#	Indicators	Point	Response options
Q2. Is there a website or document describing the web-based FMIS platform?	Q2.1	**Is there a website/document about the FMIS platform?**	0 1 2	No Yes (links to relevant documents only) Yes (FMIS-related website)
	Q2.2	If Yes to Q2.1 (1 or 2) > Related web link/URL		http:.........

Indicator 2 **FMIS web page**

Approach: Public finance organization or other government websites were screened to collect evidence about specific financial management information system (FMIS) web pages/portals, as well as publicly available FMIS-related documents.

Evidence: The URL of relevant website (Q2.2).

Point: 2 = There is a specific website presenting the characteristics of completed FMIS solutions, or the current status of FMIS implementation.

1 = There is only published reference document(s) about FMIS implementation.

0 = No dedicated website for publishing PF information is visible.

table continues next page

Table A.1 Key indicators *(continued)*

Questions	#	Indicators	Point	Response options
Q3. What is the source of the PF information that is published on the web?	**3**	**What is the source of PF data?**	0 1 2 3	No published PF data Static (tables from unidentified sources) Dynamic (archived docs from systems) Dynamic (data extracted from FMIS DB)
	Q3.2	If Dynamic (2 or 3) > Related web link/URL		http..........
	4	**Presence of open budget data (online, editable, free)**	0/1	No/Yes
	Q3.4	If Yes to open budget data (1) > Related web link/URL		http..........
	5	**Is system name visible in reports?**	0/1	No/Yes
	6	**Is system time stamp visible in reports?**	0/1	No/Yes
	Q3.7	If Yes to Q3.5 or Q3.6 (1) > Related web link/URL		http..........

Indicator 3   Source of PF information

Approach: The source of PF information was assessed by reviewing the links to related databases (static posting/dynamic query options).

Evidence: The URL of relevant dynamic website (Q3.2), since the linkage of PF information with a database is very important.

Point:
3 = Dynamic website (linked with FMIS/DW databases) with interactive query options to produce reports (for example, PDF, CSV, ODS, XLS, XML).
2 = Dynamic website (some linked with databases) to present data from a predefined list of publications (mainly PDF, XLS).
1 = Static website (not linked to databases) to publish information from unidentified sources (mainly in PDF format).
0 = There is no published PF information.

Indicator 4   Presence of open budget data

Approach: The format of published PF data was reviewed to assess compliance with minimum open budget data standards (online, editable, free).

Evidence: The URL of relevant website (Q3.4) for open budget data.

Point: 0 (No) / 1 (Yes)

Indicator 5   System name visible in reports

Approach: Check the visibility of the name of FMIS solution used as a basis for PF information in the reports published on the web.

Evidence: The URL of relevant website (Q3.7) with a report including the name of FMIS solution used as a basis.

Point: 0 (No) / 1 (Yes)

Indicator 6   System time stamp visible in reports

Approach: Check the visibility of the time stamp (date and time of publication) from the FMIS that is used as a basis for publishing reports.

Evidence: The URL of relevant website (Q3.7) with a report including the time stamp from related FMIS solution/database.

Point: 0 (No) / 1 (Yes)

table continues next page

Table A.1 Key indicators (continued)

Questions	#	Indicators	Point	Response options
Q4. Is the PF information meaningful to citizens or budget entities?	7	**Quality: What is the quality of PF data presentation?**	0	Below desired level (not informative)
			1	Partially acceptable (some useful data)
			2	Good quality (informative+easy to read)
Q4.2	8	**Content: Is there a sufficient level of detail?**	0/1	No/Yes
Q4.3	9	**Citizens Budget: Are the budget results presented easy to understand?**	0	No
			1	Yes (basic info)
			2	Yes (comprehensive info/interactive)
Q4.4		If Yes to Q4.3 on CB (1 or 2) > Related web link/URL		http:.........

Indicator 7 Quality of presentation

Evidence: Perception of the external reviewers about the overall quality of presenting open budget data. This indicator should be used with caution, since there is always a possibility of missing features that may not be so obvious while surfing relevant websites the first time.

Point: 2 = Good quality (presented reports are informative and easy to access and read).
1 = Partially acceptable (some of the published PF info is useful).
0 = Below desired level (most of the published PF info is not informative).

Indicator 8 Level of detail

Evidence: Perception of the external reviewers about the general level of detail in published reports. This indicator should be used with caution, since there is always a possibility of missing features that may not be so obvious while surfing relevant websites the first time.

Point: 0 (No) / 1 (Yes)

Indicator 9 Citizens Budget

Approach: Citizens Budget websites were screened to identify good practices where budget data are presented in meaningful format.

Evidence: The URL of relevant website (Q4.4).

Point: 2 = Yes (Comprehensive information in meaningful format for the citizens. Highly interactive.)
1 = Yes (Basic information about the budget cycle and some results in meaningful format).
0 = No

Q5. Is the data structure or full listing of budget classification (BC)/chart of accounts (CoA) published?	Q5.1	10	**Are the BC/CoA details published?**	0/1	No/Yes
	Q5.2		If Yes to Q5.1 (1) > Related web link/URL		http:.........

Indicator 10 Budget classification/chart of accounts

Approach: The PF websites were screened to spot the BC/CoA details and the revision history, as a basis for published PF data.

Evidence: The URL of relevant website (Q5.2).

Point: 0 (No) / 1 (Yes)

table continues next page

Table A.1 Key indicators *(continued)*

Questions	#	Indicators	Point	Response options
Q6. Are documents associated with annual budget plans published?	Q6.1	**Is the approved annual budget published?**	0/1	No/Yes
	Q6.2	**If Yes to Q6.1 (1): Regularity of publication**	0	Not regular
			1	Published regularly (within last 5 years)
	Q6.3	Since	Year	Starting year of publication

Indicator 11 Publishing annual budget

Evidence: Check the publication of approved annual budget documents on PF websites.
Point: 0 (No) / 1 (Yes)

Indicator 12 Regularity of publishing annual budget

Evidence: Check regular (annual) publication of annual budgets, at least within the last 5 years. Indicate the start year (Q6.3) of publications.
Point: 0 (Not regular) / 1 (Published regularly)

Questions	#	Indicators	Point	Response options
Q7. Are documents associated with medium-term expenditure framework (MTEF) published?	Q7.1	**Are MTEF documents published?**	0/1	No/Yes
	Q7.2	**If Yes to Q7.1 (1): Regularity of publication**	0	Not regular
			1	Published regularly (within last 5-yr)
	Q7.3	Period	3/5	Period (in years) of the MTEF
	Q7.4	Since	Year	Starting year of publication

Indicator 13 Publishing MTEF

Evidence: Check the publication of multiyear expenditure framework documents. Indicate the period (Q7.3) of publications.
Point: 0 (No) / 1 (Yes)

Indicator 14 Regularity of publishing MTEF

Evidence: Check regular (annual) publication of MTEF documents, at least within the last 5 years. Indicate the start year (Q7.4) of publications.
Point: 0 (Not regular) / 1 (Published regularly)

Questions	#	Indicators	Point	Response options
Q8. Are documents associated with public investment/capital budget plans published?	Q8.1	**Are public investment plans published?**	0/1	No/Yes
	Q8.2	**If Yes to Q8.1 (1): Regularity of publication**	0	Not regular
			1	Published regularly (within last 5-yr)
	Q8.3	Since	Year	Starting year of publication

Indicator 15 Public investment plans

Evidence: Check the publication of public investment plans on PF websites.
Point: 0 (No) / 1 (Yes)

table continues next page

Table A.1 Key indicators *(continued)*

Questions	#	Indicators	Point	Response options

Indicator 16   Regularity of publishing public investment plans

Evidence: Check regular (annual) publication of public investment plans, at least within the last 5 years. Indicate the start year (Q8.3) of reports.

Point: 0 (Not regular) / 1 (Published regularly)

Q9. Are documents associated with budget execution published?	Q9.1	**Are budget execution reports published?**	0/1	No/Yes
	Q9.2	If Yes to Q9.1 (1): Frequency of major publications	1 2 3 4	Weekly Monthly Quarterly Annually
	Q9.3	**18 If Yes to Q9.1 (1): Regularity of major publications**	0 1	Not regular Published regularly (within last 5-yr)
	Q9.4	Since	Year	Starting year of publication

Indicator 17   Budget execution results

Approach: The PF websites were screened to spot budget execution results mainly based on economic, administrative, and functional classification.

Evidence: Check the publication of budget execution results on PF websites, considering their frequency (Q9.2) and regularity.

Point: 0 (No) / 1 (Yes)

Indicator 18   Regularity of publishing budget execution results

Evidence: Check regular (annual) publication of budget execution results, at least within the last 5 years. Indicate the start year (Q9.4) of reports.

Point: 0 (Not regular) / 1 (Published regularly)

Q10. Are documents associated with the external audit of central government budget operations published?	Q10.1	**19 Is the external audit of central government budget operations published?**	0/1	No/Yes
	Q10.2	**20 If Yes to Q10.1 (1): Regularity of publication**	0 1	Not regular Published regularly (within last 5-yr)
	Q10.3	Since	Year	Starting year of publication

Indicator 19   External audit of budget operations

Evidence: Check the publication of external audit reports about budget operations on PF websites. Indicate the start year (Q10.3) of reports.

Point: 0 (No) / 1 (Yes)

Indicator 20   Regularity of publishing external audit reports

Evidence: Check regular (annual) publication of external audit reports about budget operations, at least within the last 5 years.

Point: 0 (Not regular) / 1 (Published regularly)

Table A.2 Informative indicators

Questions	#	Indicators	Point	Response Options
Q11. What is the level of detail of the public expenditure/revenue information published online (plans versus actuals, sectoral or regional details, and so on)?	Q11.1 / **21**	**Consolidated budget results published?**	0/1	No/Yes
	Q11.2 / 22	Sector analysis published?	0/1	No/Yes
	Q11.3 / 23	Regional analysis published?	0/1	No/Yes
	Q11.4 / 24	Gender analysis published?	0/1	No/Yes
	Q11.5 / 25	Analysis of spending for children & youth published?	0/1	No/Yes
	Q11.6 / 26	Debt data published?	0/1	No/Yes
	Q11.7 / 27	Foreign aid/grants published?	0/1	No/Yes
	Q11.8 / 28	Fiscal data on subnational government/municipalities published?	0/1	No/Yes
	Q11.9 / 29	Financial statements published?	0/1	No/Yes
	Q11.10 / 30	Public procurement and contracts published?	0/1	No/Yes
	Q11.11	Other PF data?	0/1	No/Yes
	Q11.12	If Yes to Q11.11 (1) > Related web link/URL		http……….

Indicators 21 to 30   Public expenditures > Analysis of various dimensions of budget spending

Approach: Reports on public spending were scanned further to locate specific information on (i) consolidated budget results; (ii) sectoral spending; (iii) regional spending; (iv) gender budget; (v) children's budget; (vi) debt data; (vii) aid data; (viii) fiscal data on subnational governments; (ix) financial statements; (x) public procurement and contracts; and (xi) other PF data, together with its URL (Q11.12).

Evidence: Check the publication of specific publications on various subcategories of public expenditures.

Point: 0 (No) / 1 (Yes) <<< Please note that Other PF Data (Q11.11) is included for additional information only (without a Point).

Questions	#	Indicators	Point	Response Options
Q12. Is there an open government portal?	Q12.1 / **31**	**Open government/open budget website?**	0/1	No/Yes
	Q12.2	If Yes to Q12.1 (1) > Related web link/URL		http……….

Indicator 31   Open government/open budget website

Evidence: Check the presence of open government or open budget websites, and include the URL of relevant website (Q12.2).

Point: 0 (No) / 1 (Yes)

Questions	#	Indicators	Point	Response Options
Q13. Is there a web-based system supporting the SNG PFM needs as a part of FMIS solution?	Q13.1 / **32**	**Does FMIS support the PFM needs of state/ local governments or municipalities?**	0 / 1 / 2	No / Yes (only data collection/ consolidation) / Yes (support SNG automation needs)
	Q13.2	If Yes to Q13.1 (1 or 2) > Related web link/URL		http……….

table continues next page

143

Table A.2 Informative indicators (continued)

Questions	#	Indicators	Point	Response Options
Indicator 32		**Support to subnational government operations from FMIS**		
Evidence:		Check the support to subnational government (SNG) operations from centralized FMIS, and indicate the URL of relevant website (Q13.2).		
Point:		2 = Yes (Centralized FMIS solution supports the decentralized SNG automation, data collection, and reporting needs.)		
		1 = Yes (FMIS solution provides data collection and consolidation capabilities for the SNGs).		
		0 = No		
Q14. Is there a harmonized accounting system for all budget levels (unified BC/CoA)?	**33**	**Is there a harmonized public accounting system for central + state/local governments and municipalities?**	0/1	No/Yes
		Q14.2 If Yes to Q14.1 (1) > Related web link/URL		http:.........
Indicator 33		**Harmonized accounting system for SNG**		
Evidence:		Check the presence of harmonized accounting standards for recording and reporting SNG operations, and indicate the URL of relevant website (Q14.2).		
Point:		0 (No) / 1 (Yes)		
Q15. Are there other government websites reporting budget results/performance (for example, Office of Statistics)?	**34**	**Are PF data published on the Statistics website? Or another website?**	0/3	(please see explanations below)
		Q15.2 If Q15.1 = 0 or 1 > URL of the statistics home page		http:.........
		Q15.3 Official name of statistical organization		Official name of statistics office
		Q15.4 URL of the central bank home page		http:.........
		Q15.5 Official name of central bank		Official name of central bank
		Q15.6 If Q15.1 = 2 or 3 > URL of other major alternative PF publication website		http:.........
Indicator 34		**Other PF publication websites**		
Evidence:		Check the existence of other websites (Statistics, Central Bank or other) publishing PF information, and include the URLs of relevant websites (Q15.2, Q15.4, and Q15.6). The URLs and original names of statistics organization and central bank are included as references.		
Point:		3 = Both Statistics and other websites publish PF data.		
		2 = Other website publishing PF data (no Statistics website publishing PF data).		
		1 = Statistics website publishing PF data.		
		0 = Statistics website has no PF data.		
Q16. Is there a website explaining the policy/regulations for access to PF information, web publishing standards, or frequency of reporting?	**35**	**Access to information explained?**	0/1	No/Yes
		Q16.2 If Yes to Q16.1 (1) > Related web link/URL		http:.........

table continues next page

Table A.2 Informative indicators *(continued)*

Questions	#	Indicators	Point	Response Options
Indicator 35		**Access to information**		
Evidence:		Check the presence of dedicated websites providing links or explanations about citizens' rights for access to PF information, and include the URL of relevant website (Q16.2).		
Point:		0 (No) / 1 (Yes)		
Q17. Is there a website with links to regulations for clarifying PFM roles and responsibilities?	**36**	Q17.1 **Are PFM roles/responsibilities clearly explained?**	0/1	No/Yes
		Q17.2 If Yes to Q17.1 (1) > Related web link/URL		http..........
Indicator 36		**Regulations on PFM roles and responsibilities**		
Evidence:		Check the presence of web pages providing links or explanations about PFM roles and responsibilities, and include the URL of relevant website (Q17.2).		
Point:		0 (No) / 1 (Yes)		
Q18. Are published PF data compliant with the IMF GFS and/or UN COFOG standards?	**37**	Q18.1 **Compliance with specific int'l reporting standards?**	0/2	*(please see explanations below)*
		Q18.2 If Other > Please describe reporting formats		Other reporting formats
Indicator 37		**Reporting standards**		
Evidence:		Check the availability of published budget reports in line with IMF GFS or COFOG. Indicate other reporting standards in Q18.2, if any.		
Point:		2 = IMF GFS reports are published (including UN COFOG-based functional classification of expenditures).		
		1 = Expenditure reports according to UN COFOG functional classification.		
		0 = Budget reports compliant with national standards only.		
Q19. Is there a web page for receiving feedback on PF information/user satisfaction, or for presenting web statistics?	**38**	Q19.1 **Web statistics** (for example, visitors, freq visited web pages)	0/1	No/Yes
	39	Q19.2 **Which platforms are available for feedback provision?**	0/3	*(please see explanations below)*
		Q19.3 If Other > Please describe other feedback options		Other feedback mechanisms
Indicator 38		**Web statistics (reports on website traffic)**		
Evidence:		Check the existence of web monitoring tools (web statistics and usage reports).		
Point:		0 (No) / 1 (Yes)		

table continues next page

Table A.2 Informative indicators *(continued)*

Questions		#	Indicators	Point	Response Options
Indicator 39	**Feedback/monitoring**				
Evidence:	Check the existence of feedback provision and web traffic monitoring in PF websites. Indicate other feedback mechanisms separately in Q19.3.				
Point:	3 = A number of feedback/monitoring options are visible (telephone/chat/fax/mail/e-mail/feedback forms/web statistics).				
	2 = Interactive feedback options are visible (telephone/chat/fax/mail).				
	1 = Static feedback options are available (e-mail/feedback forms/web stats).				
	0 = Not visible or inadequate.				
Q20. What languages are used to publish PF information online for external viewers?		**40**	**What is the native language?**		Enter language code (ISO 639-2 alpha-3)
		Q20.1			
		Q20.2	Language #1 option?		Indicate language #1 code
		Q20.3	Language #2 option?		Indicate language #2 code
		Q20.4	Language #3 option?		Indicate language #3 code
		Q20.5	Change of contents for PF data in other languages	0	Less detail
				1	Same level of detail in other languages
Indicator 40	**Language**				
Evidence:	Indicate the code (ISO 639-2 alpha-3) of publication language(s).				
Point:	Not used. > For Q20.5, Check if the level of detail is different in other languages >>> 0 (Less detail) / 1 (Same level of detail)				

Description of the FMIS & OBD Data Set

The data set developed for assessing the effects of financial management information systems (FMIS) on publishing open budget data is composed of five components (Figure B.1).

Key and informative indicators are explained in Appendix A.

Other components are described below:

Figure B.1 FMIS & Open Budget Data (OBD) data set

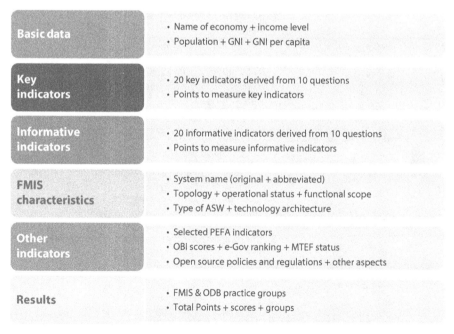

Basic data	• Name of economy + income level • Population + GNI + GNI per capita
Key indicators	• 20 key indicators derived from 10 questions • Points to measure key indicators
Informative indicators	• 20 informative indicators derived from 10 questions • Points to measure informative indicators
FMIS characteristics	• System name (original + abbreviated) • Topology + operational status + functional scope • Type of ASW + technology architecture
Other indicators	• Selected PEFA indicators • OBI scores + e-Gov ranking + MTEF status • Open source policies and regulations + other aspects
Results	• FMIS & ODB practice groups • Total Points + scores + groups

Source: World Bank data.
Note: FMIS = Financial Management Information System; GNI = Gross National Income; PEFA = Public Expenditure and Financial Accountability; OBI = Open Budget Index; MTEF = Medium-Term Expenditure Framework.

Table B.1 Basic data

Data field	Description	Values	
Economy	Name of economy + flag	Web link to related Wikipedia page	
Level	Income levels according to GNIPC (2011)	LIC	Low income	[US$1,025 or less]
		LMIC	Lower-middle income	[US$1,026 to US$4,035]
		UMIC	Upper-middle income	[US$4,036 to US$12,475]
		HIC	High income	[US$12,476 or more]
Population	Population (2011)	in thousands	
GNI	Gross National Income (2011)	in millions of USS (Atlas method)	
GNIPC	GNI per Capita (2011)	US$ (Atlas method and PPP)	

Table B.2 FMIS characteristics

Data field	Description	Values	
FMIS/TS	Abbreviation	Abbreviated name of FMIS or Treasury System	
FMIS	Full name	Full name of FMIS or TS in original language	
Topology	PFM topology	C	Centralized PFM operations
		D	Decentralized PFM operations
Functionality	FMIS functional scope	B	Budget planning/formulation (MTEF, program/ performance based budgeting)
		T	Treasury (public expenditure management)
		F	FMIS F = T + B (+O)
		O	Other FMIS components (procurement, human resources/payroll)
Status	FMIS implementation status (details of some of the systems are given as comments in related cells)	0	T/F was not implemented or not operational
		1	T/F is fully/partially operational
		2	T/F is operational for pilot or reduced-scope impl
		3	Implementation in progress
		4	Pipeline project
Op Yr	Operational year of FMIS	Year in which the FMIS/TS became operational	
Scope	Coverage of budget levels (subnational not included)	C	Only central government
		C+L	Central and Local (district) level budgets
Type	Type of FMIS project	1	T/F designed+impl as a new turnkey solution (first time or replacing previous system)
		2	Existing T/F improved or expanded
		3	New T/F implemented during emergency TA
		4	Existing T/F improved or expanded during emergency TA
		5	Improvement or expansion of an existing T/F, already implemented by the Gov/other donors
		0	Not operational
ASW	Type of application software	0	Not identified yet
		1	Locally developed software (LDSW)
		2	Commercial off-the-shelf software (COTS)
ASW solution	ASW vendor/name	COTS > Name of ASW package	
		LDSW > Name of database used in developing ASW	
Arch	ASW technology architecture	CS	Client-server (distributed system/ decentralized operations)
		Web	Web-based (centralized system/ decentralized operations)

Table B.3 Other indicators

Several indicators related to budget transparency, open data, and e-governance were also included to be able to compare the findings of this study with other assessments. Additional columns were added to list the type and total number of open source policies adopted by the national and local governments in 66 economies.

Data field	Description	Values
PEFA Yr	Year of assessment	Year of the last PEFA assessment
Stat	Disclosure status of PEFA assessment report www.pefa.org	Public Publicly available Final Completed, but not publicly disclosed Draft Draft report completed; status unknown
PI-5 [PEFA]	Classification of the budget [for details and values of all indicators > www.pefa.org]	
PI-6	Comprehensiveness of information included in budget documentation	
PI-10	Public access to key fiscal information	
PI-12	Multiyear perspective in fiscal planning, expenditure policy, and budgeting	
PI-22	Timeliness and regularity of accounts reconciliation	
PI-23	Availability of information on resources received by service delivery units	
PI-24	Quality and timeliness of in-year budget reports	
PI-25	Quality and timeliness of annual financial statements	
PI-26	Scope, nature, and follow-up of external audit	
D-2	Financial information provided by donors for budgeting and reporting on project and program aid	
Avg 10	Average of 10 PEFA indicators selected for a comparison with the FMIS & OBD scores.	
Avg	Average of all 31 PEFA indicators. NR/NA/NU scores are excluded in avg calculations.	
OBI_12	2012 Open Budget Index internationalbudget.org	0 - 20 Scant or no information 21 - 40 Minimal 41 - 60 Some 61 - 80 Significant 81 - 100 Extensive information
OBI_10	2010 Open Budget Index	Same as above
OGP	Status of participation in the Open Government Partnership initiative	0 Developing commitments 1 Commitments delivered
MTEF	Status of MTEF implementation (as of 2010)	0 No MTEF 1 MTFF (medium-term fiscal framework) 2 MTBF (medium-term budget framework) 3 MTPF (medium-term performance framework) - Unknown
eGov12	UN e-Gov Ranking (2012) UNPAN e-Gov Survey	Ranking among 193 countries included in the survey, together with the values of indices used to calculate these ratings.
eGov	e-Gov index	0 - 1
eOS	e-Gov - Online Services	0 - 1
eTC	e-Gov - Telco infrastructure	0 - 1
eHC	e-Gov - Human cap dev	0 - 1

table continues next page

Table B.3 Other indicators *(continued)*

Data field	Description	Values	
Region	World Bank Region of the economy	AFR	Africa
		EAP	East Asia and Pacific
		ECA	Europe and Central Asia
		LCR	Latin America and the Caribbean
		MNA	Middle East and North Africa
		SAR	South Asia
Zone	Zone of various countries according to their membership in international organizations	EU	European Community
		EUR	Euro zone
		AME	America
		PAC	Pacific
		OTH	Other zones
OECD	OECD membership status	OECD	Member
APEC	APEC membership status	APEC	Member
Fragile	Fragile state status	Fragile	
Economies	Name of economy	—	
OSS Gov	National Open Source Policies (in 66 economies) CSIS Government Open Source Policies (2010)	M	Mandatory, where the use of OSS is required.
		R	R&D, where the use of OSS is required.
		A	Advisory, where the use of OSS is permitted.
		P	Preference, where the use of OSS is given preference.
OSS Loc	States/provinces/cities OSS policies (in 22 economies)	Same as above	
Verif date	Date of verification message received from gov officials	dd-mmm-yy (15-May-13)	

Table B.4 Results

Data field	Description	Values	
Tot Pts	Total points (20 key indicators)	0 - 26	
Score	FMIS & OBD Score	0 - 100	
Group	FMIS & OBD Practice Group	A (Highly visible)	B (Visible)
		C (Limited visibility)	D (Minimal visibility)

Overview of Fiscal Transparency Instruments

Introduction and objectives

This appendix complements the main report by summarizing the key aspects of various global norms, indices, and initiatives that have emerged in the last decade to promote fiscal transparency (FT). The objective is to clarify the differences between internationally prominent instruments and the methodology followed in this study.

Existing FT instruments can be categorized in three parts according to their functions: (a) surveys and indices, (b) standards and norms, and (c) initiatives. A short explanation of each instrument is provided through an extract from relevant websites, and further information can be found through the web links provided.

A summary table is also included to compare the important aspects of all instruments (Table C.1).

These instruments consider various dimensions in assessing fiscal/budget transparency. The methodology applied in the current study is different than the ones these instruments use. While existing instruments mainly focus on the existence and regularity of certain key budget documents published in the public domain, and on the mechanisms for public access, this study is designed to assess the source, reliability, quality, and readability of published PF information.

The purpose of the study is not to develop another FT indicator or standard. Rather, it is a stocktaking exercise, focused on less-known aspects such as the source and reliability of open data, intended to highlight some of the good practices where FMIS is the source of meaningful open budget data.

Surveys and Indices

1. *Open Budget Index (OBI)*

http://www.openbudgetindex.org

The Open Budget Survey is designed to assist civil society groups and independent researchers in understanding selected international good practice benchmarks for budget transparency and accountability, and applying them to the practices they observe in their countries. The first Open Budget Survey was released in 2006, and it has been conducted biennially since then. Currently, the Open Budget Index covers 100 countries (2012).

As explained in the 2012 report, the Survey consists of 125 questions and is completed by independent researchers in the countries assessed. Most of these questions (95) deal directly with the public availability and comprehensiveness of the eight key budget documents that governments should publish at various points of the budget cycle. The remaining 30 questions relate to opportunities for public participation in the budget process, and to the roles played by legislatures and supreme audit institutions in budget formulation and oversight. The Open Budget Index (OBI) is calculated as a simple average of the quantified responses for the 95 survey questions that are related to budget transparency, in order to allow for comparisons across countries and over time. The OBI assigns a score to each country (0–100, in five equal intervals) based on the information it makes available to the public throughout the budget process. The index assesses the availability of eight key budget documents, the quantity of information they provide, and the timeliness of their dissemination to citizens in order to provide reliable information on each country's commitment to budget transparency and accountability.

2. *PEFA PFM Assessment*
http://www.pefa.org

The PEFA PFM Performance Measurement Framework (introduced in 2005; revised in January 2011) incorporates a public finance management (PFM) performance report and a set of high-level indicators that captures the key aspects that are recognized as being critical for all countries to achieve sound PFM. The indicator identifies comprehensiveness and transparency as one of the critical dimensions of performance of an open and orderly PFM system. It seeks to measure whether the budget and whether the fiscal risk oversight are comprehensive and fiscal and budget information is accessible to the public. The indicators are scored from A to D, with A being the best and D being the lowest score.

FT-related indicators are listed below:

• **PI-5. Classification of the budget**

A robust classification system allows the tracking of spending on the following dimensions: administrative unit, economic, functional and program. Where standard international classification practices are applied, governments can report expenditure in Government Finance Statistics (GFS) format and track poverty-reducing and other selected groups of expenditure.

- **PI-6. Comprehensiveness of information included in budget documentation**

Annual budget documentation (the annual budget and budget supporting documents), as submitted to the legislature for scrutiny and approval, should allow a complete picture of central government fiscal forecasts, budget proposals, and out-turn of previous years.

- **PI-10. Public access to key fiscal information**

Transparency will depend on whether information on fiscal plans, positions, and performance of the government is easily accessible to the general public or at least the relevant interest groups.

- **PI-12. Multiyear perspective in fiscal planning, expenditure policy and budgeting**

Expenditure policy decisions have multiyear implications, and must be aligned with the availability of resources in the medium-term perspective. Countries that have effectively introduced multiannual program budgeting are likely to show good performance on most aspects of this indicator.

- **PI-22. Timeliness and regularity of accounts reconciliation**

Reliable reporting of financial information requires constant checking and verification of the recording practices of accountants—this is an important part of internal control and a foundation for good-quality information for management and for external reports.

- **PI-23. Availability of information on resources received by service delivery units**

Front-line units providing services at the community level frequently have problems in obtaining resources that were intended for their use, whether in terms of cash transfers, distribution of materials in kind or provision of centrally recruited and paid personnel. The intended resource provision may not be explicit in budget documentation, but is likely to form part of line ministries' internal budget estimates preparation.

- **PI-24. Quality and timeliness of in-year budget reports**

The ability to "bring in" the budget requires that timely and regular information on actual budget performance be available both to the ministry of finance (and Cabinet), to monitor performance and if necessary to identify new actions to get the budget back on track, and to the ministries, departments, and agencies for managing the affairs for which they are accountable. The indicator focuses on the ability to produce comprehensive reports from the accounting system on all aspects of the budget (flash reports on release of funds to ministries, departments, and agencies are not sufficient).

- **PI-25. Quality and timeliness of annual financial statements**

Consolidated year-end financial statements are critical for transparency in the PFM system. To be complete they must be based on details for all ministries, independent departments, and deconcentrated units. In addition, the ability to prepare year-end financial statements in a timely fashion is a key indicator of how well the accounting system is operating, and of the quality of records maintained.

- **PI-26. Scope, nature, and follow-up of external audit**

A high-quality external audit is an essential requirement for creating transparency in the use of public funds. Key elements of the quality of actual external audit are the scope/coverage of the audit, adherence to appropriate auditing standards including independence of the external audit institution (ref. INTOSAI and IFAC/IAASB), focus on significant and systemic PFM issues in reports, and performance of the full range of financial audit such as reliability of financial statements, regularity of transactions, and functioning of internal control and procurement systems.

- **D-2. Financial information provided by donors for budgeting and reporting on project and program aid**

Predictability of disbursement of donor support for projects and programs (below referred to only as projects) affects the implementation of specific line items in the budget.

3. *IMF Fiscal Transparency Report on Observance of Standards and Codes (ROSC)*
http://www.imf.org/external/NP/rosc/rosc.aspx

The fiscal transparency module of the ROSC documents a country's current practices, assesses compliance with the Code of Good Practices on Fiscal Transparency, and establishes country-specific priorities for improving fiscal transparency. ROSC summarizes the extent to which countries observe certain internationally recognized standards and codes. The International Monetary Fund (IMF) has recognized 12 areas and associated standards as useful for the operational work of the Fund and the World Bank: accounting; auditing; anti-money-laundering and countering the financing of terrorism; banking supervision; corporate governance; data dissemination; fiscal transparency; insolvency and creditor rights; insurance supervision; monetary and financial policy transparency; payments systems; and securities regulation. Reports summarizing countries' observance of these standards, prepared and published at the request of the member country, are used to help sharpen the institutions' policy discussions with national authorities, and in the private sector (including by rating agencies) for risk assessment. Short updates are produced regularly, and new reports are produced every few years.

Between 1999 and March 2013, 93 countries from all Regions and levels of economic development had posted their fiscal ROSCs on the IMF's Standards and Codes web page, and 29 countries had undertaken updates or complete assessments.

4. *Global Integrity Index*
http://www.globalintegrity.org/report/methodology

The Index, launched in 2004, covers 119 countries. It is based on an Integrity Indicators scorecard that assesses the existence, effectiveness, and citizen access to key governance and anticorruption mechanisms through 320 actionable indicators. A simple aggregation method is used to produce a country's aggregate scorecard. The lead researcher for the country assigns original indicator and subindicator values. Each indicator score is then averaged within its parent subcategory, producing a subcategory score. The subcategory score is in turn averaged with the other subcategory scores into a parent category score. Category scores are averaged to produce an overall country score. The Global Integrity Report groups countries into five performance "tiers" according to their aggregated score:

- Very strong (90+)
- Strong (80+)
- Moderate (70+)
- Weak (60+)
- Very weak (< 60)

Because some aspects of governance and anticorruption mechanisms are harder to measure definitively, some categories require a more complex matrix of subindicator questions than others. The categories are equally valued, even if some categories are derived from a more lengthy series of subindicators/ questions than others. Similarly, the subcategories are equally valued within their parent category.

In other words, each score (subindicators, indicator, and so on) is equally weighted with its peers addressing the same subcategory/category. However, indicators from different categories are not necessarily equally weighted. Our approach of using equally valued concepts and adding subordinate elements as needed has produced score weightings that reflect the six main conceptual categories evenly. Although we recognize the rationale for a nonequal weighting system (to give emphasis to issues of greater import), we have yet to develop a compelling defense for valuing certain categories, subcategories, or indicators more importantly than others.

5. Right to Information (RTI) Index
http://www.rti-rating.org/index.php

The RTI Rating is a system that began in 2011 for assessing the strength of the legal framework for guaranteeing the right to information in a given country. It is limited to measuring the legal framework, and does not measure quality of implementation. Currently, the Index covers 93 countries.

In some cases, countries with relatively weak laws may nonetheless be very open, because of positive implementation efforts, while even relatively strong laws cannot ensure openness if they are not implemented properly. Regardless of these outlying cases, over time a strong access to information law can contribute to advancing openness and help those using it to defend and promote the right of access to information.

At the heart of the methodology for applying the RTI Rating are 61 indicators. For each indicator, countries earn points within a set range of scores (in most cases 0–2), depending on how well the legal framework delivers the indicator, for a possible total of 150 points.

The indicators are drawn from a wide range of international standards on the right to information, as well as comparative study of numerous rights to information laws from around the world.

The indicators are grouped into the following seven main categories:

Section	Max Points
1. Right of access	6
2. Scope	30
3. Requesting procedures	30
4. Exceptions and refusals	30
5. Appeals	30
6. Sanctions and protections	8
7. Promotional measures	16
Total score	**150**

6. *UN e-Government Survey and Rankings*
http://www2.unpan.org/egovkb/global_reports/index.htm

The Global e-Government Development Survey, first released in 2003, presents a systemic assessment of how governments use information and communications technology (ICT) to provide access and inclusion for all. Each Survey offers insights into the different strategies and common themes in e-government development among and across regions. By studying broad patterns of e-government use, it identifies countries that have taken a leadership role in promoting e-government development and those where the potential of ICT for development has not yet been exploited.

The Survey aims to inform and improve the understanding of policy makers' choices in their e-government program undertakings. It is a useful tool for government officials, researchers, and the representatives of civil society and the private sector to gain a deeper understanding of the relative position of a country vis-à-vis the rest of the world's economies. In this way the Survey rankings hope to contribute to the e-government efforts of the member states as they move to provide access for all. It ranks 193 countries.

The Survey consists of four parts: information dissemination and outreach, access and usability, service delivery capability, and citizen participation and interconnectedness.

Standards and Norms

7. *IMF Code of Good Practices on Fiscal Transparency*
http://www.imf.org/external/np/pp/2007/eng/051507c.pdf

The Code identifies a set of principles and practices to help governments provide a clear picture of the structure and finances of government (released in 1998;

updated in 2007). It underpins the voluntary program of fiscal transparency assessments called ROSC fiscal transparency modules. It identifies four areas:

- Clarity of roles and responsibilities
- Open budget processes
- Public availability of information
- Assurances of integrity.

8. OECD *Best Practices for Budget Transparency*
http://www.oecd.org/dataoecd/33/13/1905258.pdf.

The Organisation for Economic Co-operation and Development (OECD) Best Practices are a reference tool issued in 2002. They support the full disclosure of all relevant fiscal information in a timely and systematic manner and provide a series of best practices in the areas of principal budget reports, specific disclosures, quality, and integrity.

The Best Practices are in three parts. Part 1 lists the principal budget reports that governments should produce, and their general content. Part 2 describes specific disclosures to be contained in the reports, including both financial and nonfinancial performance information. Part 3 highlights practices for ensuring the quality and integrity of the reports.

The Best Practices are organized around specific reports for presentational reasons only. It is recognized that different countries will have different reporting regimes and may have different areas of emphasis for transparency. The Best Practices are based on different member countries' experiences in each area. It should be stressed that the Best Practices are not meant to constitute a formal "standard" for budget transparency.

Fiscal Transparency Initiatives

9. *Global Initiative for Fiscal Transparency (GIFT)*
http://fiscaltransparency.net/

The Global Initiative for Fiscal Transparency (GIFT) was launched in 2011 as a multistakeholder action network working to advance and institutionalize global norms and significant, continuous improvements on fiscal transparency, participation, and accountability in countries around the world. GIFT aims to achieve this by advancing incentives, norms, technical assistance, and new technologies. GIFT mobilizes a wide range of stakeholders—national authorities, the private sector, civil society, and international organizations—in support of fiscal transparency initiatives at the global and national levels.

At the global level, GIFT seeks to strengthen the normative framework for fiscal transparency by harmonizing norms and standards and addressing gaps related to participation, the role of the legislature, and open data. At the national level, GIFT facilitates multistakeholder engagement on fiscal transparency by sharing international experience and providing support to multistakeholder forums and technical advice in the implementation of their work programs.

10. *Open Government Partnership*
http://www.opengovpartnership.org

Open Government Partnership (OGP) is an international organization promoting multilateral initiatives and seeking strong commitments from participating government institutions to promote transparency, increase civic participation, fight corruption, and harness new technologies to make government more open, effective, and accountable.

This initiative was launched on September 20, 2011, with the endorsement of a declaration by eight countries (Brazil, Indonesia, Mexico, Norway, Philippines, South Africa, United Kingdom, and United States). Since then, 47 additional members have joined the group endorsing the declaration (as of June 2013); 5 other countries are expected to officially endorse the declaration in 2013, and are in the process of developing commitments.

The OGP provides an international forum for dialogue and sharing among governments, civil society organizations, and the private sector, all of which contribute to a common pursuit of open government. OGP stakeholders include participating governments as well as civil society and private sector entities that support the principles and mission of OGP.

Table C.1 Overview of fiscal transparency instruments

Category	Instrument	Number of countries	Since/updates	Stated objective	Methodology
SURVEYS AND INDICES	Open Budget Index (OBI)	94	2006 biennial last: 2010 next: 2012	To evaluate whether governments give the public access to budget information and opportunities to participate in the budget process at the national level.	http://www.openbudgetindex.org The Open Budget Survey is based on a detailed questionnaire to guide civil society researchers from each country through each of the four stages of the budget process. The questionnaire contains a total of 123 questions. The responses to 92 of the questions that evaluate public access to budget information are averaged to form the Open Budget Index. The remaining 31 questions cover topics related to opportunities for public participation in the budget process and the ability of key oversight institutions of government to hold the executive accountable.
	PEFA PFM Assessment	121 Public: 65	2005	By providing a common pool of information for measuring and monitoring PFM performance progress, and a common platform for dialogue about PFM reform, it aims to contribute to the development of effective country-owned PFM systems.	http://www.pefa.org The PEFA framework was created as a high-level analytical instrument that consists of a set of 31 indicators and a supporting PFM Performance Report, providing an overview of the performance of a country's PFM system. Drawing on the established international standards and codes and other commonly recognized good practices in PFM, it forms part of the "strengthened approach to supporting PFM reform," which emphasizes country-led reform, donor harmonization and alignment around the country strategy, and a focus on monitoring results. The indicators are scored from A to D, with A being the best and D being the lowest score.
	IMF Fiscal Transparency ROSC	93	1999	ROSCs summarize the extent to which countries observe certain internationally recognized standards and codes.	http://www.imf.org/external/NP/rosc/rosc.aspx ROSCs document a country's current practices, assess compliance with the Code of Good Practices on FT, and establish country-specific priorities for improving FT.
	Global Integrity Index	119	2004	The Global Integrity Index assesses the existence and effectiveness of, and citizen access to, key national-level anticorruption mechanisms used to hold governments accountable.	http://www.globalintegrity.org/report The Global Integrity Index is generated by aggregating more than 300 Integrity Indicators systematically gathered for each country covered. For the 2009 Global Integrity Index, those indicators comprised more than 100,000 peer-reviewed questions and answers scored by in-country experts. Several rounds of review are conducted at the international level to ensure that cross-country comparisons are valid. In addition, all assessments are reviewed by a country-specific, double-blind peer review panel comprising additional local and international subject matter experts.

table continues next page

Table C.1 Overview of fiscal transparency instruments *(continued)*

Category	Instrument	Number of countries	Since/updates	Stated objective	Methodology
	Right to Information (RTI) Index	93	2011	To assess the strength of the legal framework for guaranteeing the right to information in a given country. It is limited to measuring the legal framework, and does not measure quality of implementation.	http://www.rti-rating.org/index.php There are 61 indicators. For each indicator, countries earn points within a set range of scores (in most cases 0–2), depending on how well the legal framework delivers the indicator, for a possible total of 150 points. The indicators are drawn from a wide range of international standards on the right to information, as well as a comparative study of numerous rights to information laws from around the world.
	UN E-gov Survey and Rankings	193	2003 biennial since 2004 last: 2012	To systemically assess how governments use information and communications technology (ICT) to provide access and inclusion for the public.	http://www2.unpan.org/egovkb/global_reports/index.htm The Survey consists of four parts: information dissemination and outreach, access and usability, service delivery capability, and citizen participation and interconnectedness. Countries are ranked according to the score of the Survey.
STANDARDS AND NORMS	IMF Code of Good Practices on Fiscal Transparency	n.a.	1998 Last update: 2007	To identify a set of principles and practices to help governments provide a clear picture of the structure and finances of government.	http://www.imf.org/external/np/pp/2007/eng/051507c.pdf It identifies four areas: clarity of roles and responsibilities, open budget processes, public availability of information, and assurances of integrity. Another update, initiated in 2012, is under way. Best Practices for Budget Transparency
	OECD	n.a.	2002	To support the full disclosure of all relevant fiscal information in a timely and systematic manner and provide a series of best practices in the areas of principal budget reports, specific disclosures, quality, and integrity.	http://www.oecd.org/dataoecd/33/13/1905258.pdf The Best Practices are in three parts. Part 1 lists the principal budget reports that governments should produce and their general content. Part 2 describes specific disclosures to be contained in the reports, including both financial and nonfinancial performance information. Part 3 highlights practices for ensuring the quality and integrity of the reports. The Best Practices are based on different member countries' experiences in each area; they are not meant to constitute a formal "standard" for budget transparency.

table continues next page

Table C.1 Overview of fiscal transparency instruments *(continued)*

Category	Instrument	Number of countries	Since/updates	Stated objective	Methodology
INITIATIVES	Global Initiative for Fiscal Transparency (GIFT)	n.a.	2011	To contribute to significant, continuous improvements on fiscal transparency, public participation, and accountability by advancing incentives, norms, technical assistance, and new technologies.	http://fiscaltransparency.net GIFT mobilizes a wide range of stakeholders. At the global level, GIFT seeks to strengthen the normative framework for fiscal transparency by harmonizing norms and standards and addressing gaps related to participation, the role of the legislature, and open data. At the national level, GIFT facilitates the multistakeholder engagement on fiscal transparency by sharing international experience and providing support to multistakeholder forums and technical advice in the implementation of their work programs.
	Open Government Partnership	55 committed 5 in progress	2011	To promote transparency, increase civic participation, fight corruption, and harness new technologies to make government more open, effective, and accountable.	http://www.opengovpartnership.org Open Government Partnership (OGP) provides an international forum for dialogue and sharing among governments, civil society organizations, and the private sector, all of which contribute to a common pursuit of open government. OGP stakeholders include participating governments as well as civil society and private sector entities that support the principles and mission of OGP.

Source: World Bank data.

Note: IMF = International Monetary Fund; OECD = Organisation for Economic Co-operation and Development; PEFA = Public Expenditure and Financial Accountability; PFM = Public financial management; n.a. = not applicable.

APPENDIX D

Feedback Providers

The feedback provided by the following government officials (Table D.1) on the initial findings of this study was very useful to improve the quality of the data set and the evidence collected. The authors are grateful to all government officials (from 43 economies) for their valuable support. The team would also like to express sincere appreciation to the World Bank staff and other financial management information systems (FMIS) Community of Practice members who assisted in the coordination of efforts and collection of responses on the FMIS and Open Budget Data survey.

Table D.1 Feedback providers

Economy	Government officials	The World Bank staff	Others (FMIS CoP)
Albania	Odeta Kromici	Evis Sulko	
Argentina	Raul Rigo	Mamadou Deme, Alejandro Solanot	
Armenia	Grigor Aramyan	Davit Melikyan	
Azerbaijan	Nazim Gasimzade		
Bangladesh	Ranjit Chakraborty	Dilshad Dossani, Jonas Fallov	
Barbados	Juanita Thorington-Powlett, Nancy Headley		
Belize	Zita Magana Perez		
Botswana	Grace Nkateng		
Colombia	David Morales	Jeannette Estupinan	
	Shirley Herreño		
	Oscar E. Escobar		
	Eduardo Rodriguez		
Croatia	Marijana Müller		
Cyprus	Maria Dionysiou		
El Salvador	Lilena Martínez de Soto		
Finland	Marko Oja, Economics Dept.		
Ghana	Sammy Arkhurst	Ismaila Ceesay	
Hong Kong SAR, China	Thebe Ng		
Indonesia	MoF officials	Hari Purnomo	

table continues next page

Table D.1 Feedback providers (continued)

Economy	Government officials	The World Bank staff	Others (FMIS CoP)
Ireland	Joe Kirwan, John Palmer, Dept of Finance		Thomas Ferris
Republic of Korea	Hyangwoo Jeong, Ji-yeon Kim		
Kyrgyz Republic	Nurida Baizakova	Zhanybek Ybraiym Uulu	
Lao PDR	Sifong Oumavong	Minh Van Nguyen	
Latvia	Sintija Dadzīte		
Lithuania	Grazina Steponenaite		
Madagascar	MoF officials	Anne-Lucie Lefebvre, Haja Andriamarofara	
Mauritius	R. Kalleechurn		
Myanmar	MoF Budget Department		
Netherlands	Rense Posthumus		
New Zealand	Nicola Haslam, Emma Taylor		Ian Storkey
Nicaragua	MoF officials	Daniela Felcman, Alberto Leyton	
Norway	Pål Ulla		
Paraguay	María Teresa de Agüero	Mamadou Deme	
Poland	Piotr Dragańczuk	Iwona Warzecha	
Russian Federation	Renold Rubies	Irina Rostovtseva	
San Marino	Roberta Mularoni		
Singapore	Wang Shihui		
Slovak Republic	Katarína Kováčová		
Slovenia	Senka Maver, Vesna Derenčin		
Solomon Islands	Norman Hiropuhi	Timothy Bulman	
South Sudan	David Martin	Parminder Brar, Adenike Oyeyiola	
Spain	Carmen Castaño		
Tajikistan	MoF officials	Hassan Aliev	
Ukraine	Roman Chuprynenko, Konstantin Stanytskyy	Tetiana Kovalchuk	
United States of America	Dustin Brown, Regina Kearney	Joanna Watkins	
Vietnam	MoF officials	Quyen Vu, Khanh Linh Thi Le	

Bibliography

Dener, Cem, Joanna A. Watkins, and William L. Dorotinsky. 2011. *Financial Management Information Systems: 25 Years of World Bank Experience on What Works and What Doesn't.* World Bank Study. Washington, DC: World Bank.

International Budget Partnership. 2011. *A Guide to Transparency in Public Finances: Looking Beyond the Budget.* International Budget Partnership.

———. 2012. *The Power of Making It Simple: A Government Guide to Developing Citizens Budgets.* Includes five briefs that go beyond the eight key budget reports covered in the guide:

- Extrabudgetary Funds
- Tax Expenditures
- Quasi-Fiscal Activities
- Contingent Liabilities
- Future Liabilities

International Monetary Fund. 2012. *Data Quality Assessment Framework for Government Finance Statistics.* Washington, DC: IMF.

———. 2012. *Fiscal Transparency, Accountability, and Risk.* Washington, DC: IMF.

Manning, Nick, Geoffrey Shepherd, and Alejandro Guerrero. 2010. "Why Trust in Government Matters?" In *Results, Performance Budgeting and Trust in Government.* Washington, DC: World Bank.

National Coalition for Dialogue & Deliberation. 2009. *The Core Principles for Public Engagement.*

National Consumer Council. 2008. *Deliberative Public Engagement: Nine Principles.*

Padgett, John F., and Walter W. Powell. 2012. *The Emergence of Organizations and Markets.* Princeton: Princeton University Press. (review of the book).

Public Expenditure and Financial Accountability (PEFA) Program.

Supreme Audit Institutions Performance Measurement Framework (SAI-PMF), Draft Version 2.0, September 2012.

World Bank FMIS Database (1984–2013), updated July 2013.

Open Data References

Creative Commons (CC) Licenses for Open Source: http://creativecommons.org.

G8 Open Data Charter; Improving the transparency and accountability of government and its services, 18 June 2013.

List of open data catalogs: http://www.datacatalogs.org.

Open Data Handbook: http://opendatahandbook.org.

Open Knowledge Foundation Open Data Guide: http://opendatacommons.org/guide.

Open Knowledge Foundation Guide: http://opengovernmentdata.org.

Publishing Open Government Data: http://www.w3.org/TR/gov-data.

Putting Government Data Online: http://www.w3.org/DesignIssues/GovData.html.

UN DevInfo: http://www.devinfo.org.

World Bank Open Data portal: http://data.worldbank.org.

World Bank Open Government Data Toolkit (OGD Toolkit), released in Nov 2012: http://data.worldbank.org/open-government-data-toolkit.

World Wide Web Foundation, Open Gov Data: http://webfoundation.org/projects/ogd.

Environmental Benefits Statement

The World Bank is committed to reducing its environmental footprint. In support of this commitment, the Publishing and Knowledge Division leverages electronic publishing options and print-on-demand technology, which is located in regional hubs worldwide. Together, these initiatives enable print runs to be lowered and shipping distances decreased, resulting in reduced paper consumption, chemical use, greenhouse gas emissions, and waste.

The Publishing and Knowledge Division follows the recommended standards for paper use set by the Green Press Initiative. Whenever possible, books are printed on 50% to 100% postconsumer recycled paper, and at least 50% of the fiber in our book paper is either unbleached or bleached using Totally Chlorine Free (TCF), Processed Chlorine Free (PCF), or Enhanced Elemental Chlorine Free (EECF) processes.

More information about the Bank's environmental philosophy can be found at http://crinfo.worldbank.org/wbcrinfo/node/4.

www.ingramcontent.com/pod-product-compliance
Lightning Source LLC
Chambersburg PA
CBHW080412060326
40689CB00019B/4223